SpringerBriefs in Economics

Kobe University Social Science Research Series

The Kobe University Social Science Research Series has been established as a subseries of the SpringerBrief in Economics Series, but in fact this exciting interdisciplinary collection encompasses scholarly research not only in the economics but also in law, political science, business and management, accounting, international relations, and other subdisciplines within the social sciences. As a national university with a special strength in the social sciences, Kobe University actively promotes interdisciplinary research. This series is not limited only to research emerging from Kobe University's faculties of social sciences but also welcomes cross-disciplinary research that integrates studies in the arts and sciences.

Kobe University, founded in 1902, is the second oldest national higher education institution for commerce in Japan and is now a preeminent institution for social science research and education in the country. Currently, the social sciences section includes four faculties—Law, Economics, Business Administration, and International Cooperation Studies—and the Research Institute for Economics and Business Administration (RIEB). There are some 230-plus researchers who belong to these faculties and conduct joint research through the Center for Social Systems Innovation and the Organization for Advanced and Integrated Research, Kobe University.

This book series comprises academic works by researchers in the social sciences at Kobe University as well as their collaborators at affiliated institutions, Kobe University alumni and their colleagues, and renowned scholars from around the world who have worked with academic staff at Kobe University. Although traditionally the research of Japanese scholars has been publicized mainly in the Japanese language, Kobe University strives to promote publication and dissemination of works in English in order to further contribute to the global academic community.

More information about this series at http://www.springer.com/series/15423

Tomoko Kinugasa · Linhui Yu
Qiang Chen · Zhixuan Feng

Economic Growth and Transition of Industrial Structure in East Asia

Springer

Tomoko Kinugasa
Graduate School of Economics
Kobe University
Kobe, Hyōgo, Japan

Qiang Chen
School of Economics
Shandong University
Jinan, Shandong, China

Linhui Yu
School of Economics
Zhejiang University
Hangzhou, China

Zhixuan Feng
School of Economics
Nankai University
Tianjin, China

ISSN 2191-5504 ISSN 2191-5512 (electronic)
SpringerBriefs in Economics
ISSN 2520-1697 ISSN 2520-1700 (electronic)
Kobe University Social Science Research Series
ISBN 978-981-13-2867-1 ISBN 978-981-13-2868-8 (eBook)
https://doi.org/10.1007/978-981-13-2868-8

Library of Congress Control Number: 2018957670

This Springer imprint is published by the registered company Springer Nature Singapore Pte Ltd.
The registered company address is: 152 Beach Road, #21-01/04 Gateway East, Singapore 189721, Singapore

Preface

Many East Asian countries have experienced dramatic economic growth since the World War II, and a tremendous amount of change has since been observed in the industrial structure. East Asia has seen remarkable economic growth, which has been dubbed as the "East Asian miracle" by the World Bank. The dramatic economic growth could be related to remarkable industrialization. Before the World War II, most of the global population was engaged in agriculture. In the dual-sector models proposed by Lewis (1954) and Ranis and Fei (1961), agriculture is the primary industry in the early stage of economic development. Economies develop further when the labor force moves from an agrarian sector to a manufacturing one. As Asian countries developed, manufacturing became the main industry, and soon afterward, the overall share of service industries in the economy increased. At present, there are many developed industries such as the high-tech and IT industries.

A notable point is that rapid demographic transition was experienced in East Asian countries in the latter half of the 20th century. Before this transition occurred, both fertility and mortality rates were high. As countries developed, mortality, particularly infant mortality, began to decline rapidly. This was followed by a rapid decline in fertility as well. During the demographic transition, the proportion of working-age individuals in the population increased drastically. As per the demographic dividend reported by Bloom and Williamson (1998), this favorable demographic situation, with its higher share of the working-age population and fewer individuals belonging to the dependent population, contributed to remarkable economic growth in Asia.

Moreover, it is widely considered that globalization has substantially contributed to economic growth in East Asia. Numerous globalization trends have been noted. In particular, the General Agreement on Tariffs and Trade (GATT) was established in 1947 to liberalize worldwide trade. However, the GATT ceased to exist after the World Trade Organization (WTO) was established in 1995. This has led to the further promotion of trade liberalization and regional economic integration on a global scale. In Southeast Asia, Association of Southeast Asian Nations (ASEAN) was established in 1967, and free trade was promoted among the member countries. Many kinds of free trade agreements (FTAs) and economic partnership agreements (EPAs) have been acknowledged, and international trade has expanded dramatically.

The abovementioned changes are largely inter-related, and there is further scope for research in these domains. This book tries to explore the new frontier of research in economic growth and industrial reconstructing. First, the demographic effects on trade have not been analyzed in depth in any previous research; Chap. 1 tries to explore these effects. The research presented in Chap. 1 elucidates the effects of demographic change on trade openness and trade balance. Second, as a country develops and undergoes industrialization, remarkable urbanization is observed. Large cities experience economies and diseconomies of agglomeration. Chapter 2 presents the first research that discusses the agglomeration economies and diseconomies between firms and workers and provides empirical evidence for the misallocation of agglomeration economies and diseconomies in China. Third, economic growth and industrial construction are related to historical events. Just considering the present situation would not suffice, and it is important to discuss history in the long run. Before the era of industrialization, agriculture and stock-breeding were the primary industries, and there were frequent conflicts between the nomadic and agricultural people. Chapter 3 focuses on the dynastic cycles observed in China as well as countries near China and investigates the determinants of conquests by nomadic people. An interesting finding was that an older nomadic regime was more likely to be conquered by a younger nomadic regime. This research could provide a basic rationale behind the rise and fall of national power. Fourth, characteristics of exchange, particularly in the context of international exchange, have not been sufficiently analyzed in previous studies but appear to be quite important during the transition era characterized by remarkable economic growth and dramatic change in the industrial structure; Chap. 4 tries to explore this issue. In Chap. 4, critiques of Emmanuel's unequal exchange theory are discussed based on the data of profit in the world.

The contents of this book are summarized as follows: Chap. 1, written by Yukio Fukumoto and Tomoko Kinugasa, focuses our attention on trade and demographic change. In this chapter, using 8 panel data of APEC economies available for the period between 1951 and 2010, the authors empirically investigate whether trade openness and trade balance to GDP ratio are influenced by age structure. The authors suggest that age structure influences trade openness because education, nursing care, and medical services are mostly non-tradable, and the share of consumption for non-tradable goods is likely to be high in the dependent age. They also suggest that age structure influences trade balance because trade balance is a part of the current account balance. Furthermore, previous studies report the influence of age structure on the current account balance. The empirical results described herein suggest that the share of working-age population (dependency ratio) has a significantly positive (negative) effect on trade openness and trade balance to GDP ratio. In many APEC economies, the share of working-age population is increasing; however, the speed at which this increase is occurring varies among the economies.

Hence, Fukumoto and Kinugasa conclude that age structure has contributed to increases in trade openness and caused trade imbalances in APEC economies.

Chapter 2 is authored by Hongzhong Fan and Linhui Yu. In this chapter, through regression analysis of survey data collected from peasant workers in China, the authors reveal that nominal wages and living costs of these workers are essentially identical across cities of different sizes. This finding suggests that in developing countries with conspicuous and sustained employment pressures like China, the bargaining power of low-skilled workers are so weak that they have no leverage in transferring the high costs of living in large cities to their employers by demanding better nominal wages. As a result, firms in large cities enjoy most of the benefits afforded by agglomeration at disproportionately reduced costs. In contrast, low-skilled workers bear the costs of agglomeration without earning an equitable level of benefits from living in large cities. In this case, the market mechanism that normally operates to limit city size growth evidently fails to work, which unavoidably promotes the overexpansion of megacities.

Chapter 3 is written by Qiang Chen. This chapter is about dynastic cycles and nomadic conquests. Conflict between nomadic and agricultural people has been a recurring phenomenon throughout world history. A recent study finds that dynastic cycles are an important determinant of nomadic conquests in the context of Sino-nomadic conflict, where an aging Chinese dynasty was more likely to be conquered. This paper extends this result in two dimensions using a sample of nomads in or near China and a sample from world history. The effects of dynastic cycles on nomadic conquests remain significant in a much broader context. Overall, the dynastic cycle appears to be a general force shaping world history that has been hitherto underappreciated.

Chapter 4 is written by Zhixuan Feng. This chapter reviews the critiques on Emmanuel's unequal exchange theory and finds that a crucial concept, international value, has been neglect. Considering international value, there is no relationship between the formation of international production price that is the foundation of unequal exchange and the perfect mobility of capital among countries. An empirical estimation of equalization of profit rate based on the framework of regulation capital is used to certify this viewpoint. By introducing international value, the unequal exchange theory can survive from the critique focusing on the reality of international profit rate equalization. However, the international concept also implies that unequal exchange is not a straight result of the difference of domestic income distribution between countries, but a consequence of the international division of labor. The author also examines the existence of unequal exchange by calculating the gap between international production price and international value, i.e., the volume of transferred value of 40 countries, and finds that unequal exchange does exist and is significant enough to affect the development of one country.

This book is highly recommended for readers who would like to obtain a fresh perspective about economic development in terms of industrial structure. The main part of this book is based on the Annual Conference by Four Universities of Japan and China: Economic Growth and Industrial Restructuring of East Asia held on

December 9, 2016, and hosted by the School of Economics, Zhejiang University. We are grateful to Profs. Taiji Hagiwara, Yun Zhang, Guangjie Ning, Chicheng Ma, Takashi Yanagawa, and participants of the conference.

Kobe, Japan — Tomoko Kinugasa
Hangzhou, China — Linhui Yu
Jinan, China — Qiang Chen
Tianjin, China — Zhixuan Feng

References

Bloom D, Williamson J (1998) Demographic transitions and economic miracles in emerging Asia. World Bank Econ Rev 12:419–455

Lewis AW (1954) Economic development with unlimited supplies of labor, manchester school of economics and social studies 22:139–191

Ranis G, Fei J (1961) A theory of economic development. Am Econ Rev 51:533–565

Contents

Chapter 1
Does Demographic Change Influence International Trade?: An Empirical Study on APEC Economies

Yukio Fukumoto and Tomoko Kinugasa

Abstract Today, trade in APEC economies accounts for almost one-half of the world trade, and trade surplus in Asian economies and trade deficits in the United States are causing global trade imbalance. In this study, we empirically investigate whether trade openness and trade balance to GDP ratio are influenced by age structure, using panel data of APEC economies from 1951 to 2010. Our empirical results suggest that the share of working-age population (dependency ratio) has a significantly positive (negative) effect on trade openness and trade balance to GDP ratio. In many APEC economies, the share of working-age population is increasing and the speed varies among the economies. Hence, it is reasonable to believe that age structure has contributed to increases in trade openness and has caused trade imbalances in APEC economies.

Keywords Age structure · Trade openness · Trade balance to GDP ratio
APEC economies

1.1 Introduction

Asia-Pacific Economic Cooperation (APEC) was established in 1989, and APEC includes 21 economies in Pan Pacific. APEC has tried to develop further regional economic integration by supporting free and open trade and investment. Currently, APEC includes the world top three countries of GDP: United States, China, and Japan and is the largest regional group in the world; in APEC, GDP accounts for 60%, international trade accounts for 50%, population accounts for 40% of the world. In Asia and North America, which include major APEC economies, the share of trade within the area in total trade is quite high.[1] The share of Asia's trade flows in Asia's total merchandise exports is 52.3% and that of North America's trade flows in North America's total merchandise exports is 50.2%. Moreover, the share of Asia's trade

[1] Data source is from intra- and inter-regional merchandise trade, 2014 (Table I.4), in International trade statistics 2015 published by the World Trade Organization. It is available at https://www.wto.org/english/res_e/statis_e/its2015_e/its15_world_trade_dev_e.htm.

T. Kinugasa et al., *Economic Growth and Transition of Industrial Structure in East Asia*, Kobe University Social Science Research Series,
https://doi.org/10.1007/978-981-13-2868-8_1

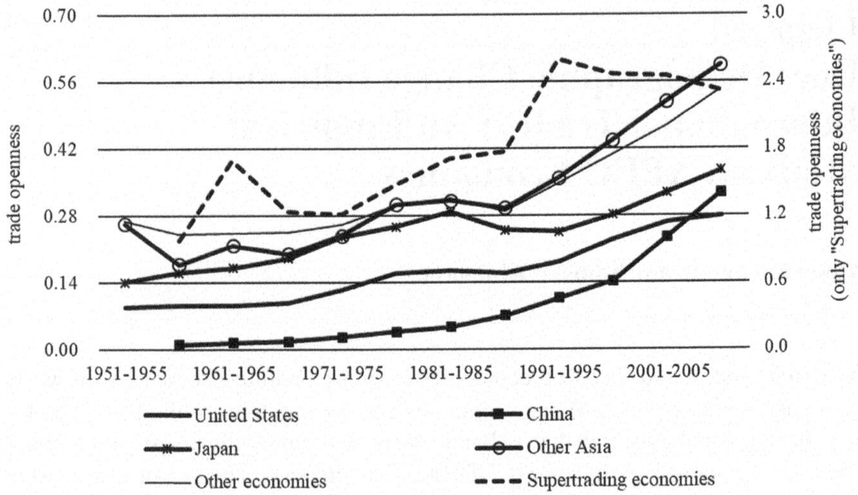

Fig. 1.1 Trade openness in APEC economies. *Note* The data source is *Penn World Table 8.0*. For details, see Sect. 1.3. Five-year average data from 1951 to 2010 are used. Other Asia includes six APEC economies: Indonesia, the Philippines, the Republic of Korea, Taiwan, Thailand, and Viet Nam. Other economies include seven APEC economies: Australia, Canada, Chile, Mexico, New Zealand, Peru, and Russia. Supertrading economies include three APEC economies: Hong Kong, Malaysia, and Singapore. Other Asia, Other economies, and Supertrading economies are calculated as simple arithmetic average values of sample economies

flows in North America's total merchandise exports is 20.2% and that of North America's trade flows in Asia's total merchandise exports is 18.0%. For reference, in Europe, where the share of trade within the area is high, the share of Europe's trade flows in Europe's total merchandise export is 68.5%.

Figure 1.1 shows trade openness (i.e., the ratio of trade to GDP) in 19 APEC economies.[2] Trade openness increased in the United States, China, Japan, other Asia (Indonesia, Philippines, Republic of Korea, Taiwan, Thailand, and Viet Nam), other economies (Australia, Canada, Chile, Mexico, New Zealand, Peru, and Russia), and supertrading economies (Hong Kong, Malaysia, and Singapore).[3] In this period, many APEC economies have experienced economic growth, therefore, it could be confirmed that international trade in APEC economies has grown faster than their output. It is often pointed that international trade and economic growth have positive relationship, and it seems to hold true for APEC economies.[4]

[2]Hereafter, we deal with 19 APEC economies, and we do not consider Brunei Darussalam and Papua New Guinea because of the reason described in Sect. 1.3.

[3]Krugman (1995) named the following six economies, Singapore, Hong Kong, Malaysia, Belgium, Ireland, and Netherlands, which had quite high exports as percentage of GDP in 1990, as supertrading economies. Krugman (1995) pointed that there was no economies that can be classified as supertrading economies in globalization before World War I. See Krugman (1995, pp. 334–335).

[4]For example, Dooley et al. (2004, p. 309) insisted "…, exporting to the USA is Asia's main concern. Exports mean growth."

One of the most serious economic problems among APEC economies should be regional trade imbalance. Figure 1.2 shows trade balance to GDP ratio in 19 APEC economies. According to Fig. 1.2, trade surplus in Japan and trade deficit in the United States increased in 1980s, and trade surplus has increased in most APEC economies since the latter half of 1990s, on the other hand, trade deficit has increased further in the United States. Trade development does not necessarily increase exports and imports equally; consequently, it is possible that an increase in trade openness worsen trade imbalance to GDP ratio. Regardless of the result of individual optimization decisions, it is possible that large trade imbalance will cause political and economic conflicts among economies. Many Asian economies represented by China and Japan have increased international trade and have had huge trade surplus with the United States, so that chronic trade deficit in the United States has increased. This trade imbalance received attention as global trade imbalance.

This research tries to investigate empirically whether trade openness and trade balance to GDP ratio are influenced by age structure in APEC economies. Fukumoto and Kinugasa (2017) pointed that an increase in share of working-age population in total population raised trade openness, and Hill (1989) and Herbertsson and Zoega (1999) insisted that it induced trade surplus. Figure 1.3 shows share of working-age population in 19 APEC economies. In many APEC economies, the share of working-age population has increased since 1970s. In addition, growth rate of the share of working-age population in the United States is lower than many other APEC economies. Figures 1.1, 1.2 and 1.3 seem to be consistent with hypotheses of Fukumoto and Kinugasa (2017), Hill (1989) and Herbertsson and Zoega (1999). If demographic change influence international trade, it is probable that an increase in share of working-age population has contributed to development in trade in APEC economies. Moreover, it is reasonable that a rapid increase in share of working-age

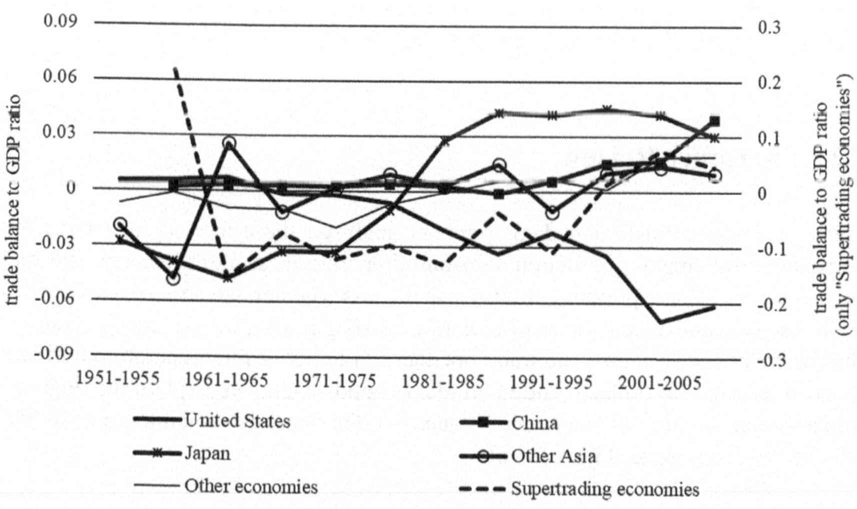

Fig. 1.2 Trade balance to GDP ratio in APEC economies. *Note* See the note of Fig. 1.1

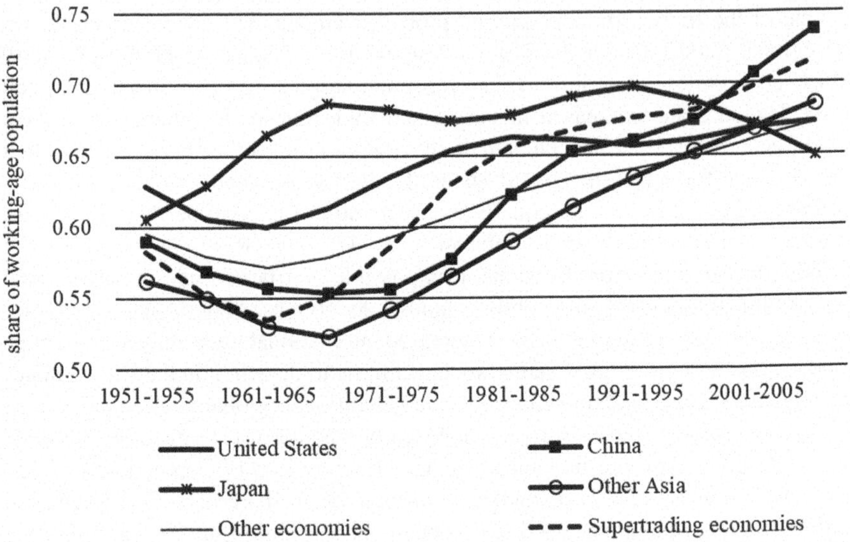

Fig. 1.3 Share of working-age population in APEC economies. *Note* The data source except for Taiwan is *World Population Prospects: The 2015 Revision*. For Taiwan, the data source is the *Human Mortality Database*. For other information, see the note of Fig. 1.1

population has increased trade surplus in Asian economies. Accordingly, trade deficit in the United States, an important trade partner of Asian economies, might have been induced.

The rest of this paper is organized as follows. In Sect. 1.2, we discuss how age structure influence trade openness and trade balance to GDP ratio, based on previous studies. In Sect. 1.3, empirical model and data used in our analyses are explained. In Sect. 1.4, empirical results are discussed. Section 1.5 draws conclusions.

1.2 Literature Review

Many macroeconomists and demographers analyzed the effects of age structure on saving, investment, production, consumption, current account balance, and real exchange rate.[5] Some previous studies also discuss whether age structure influences trade openness and trade balance to GDP ratio. To begin with, we explain the relationship between age structure and trade openness in terms of intergenerational differences of demand for tradable and nontradable goods. Next, we explain the relationship between age structure and trade balance to GDP ratio based on intergenerational differences of saving and investment.

[5]Modigliani and Brumberg (1954) is the primary research in this field.

Fukumoto and Kinugasa (2017) suggested that there exists a relationship between age structure and trade openness. They hypothesized that the consumption of dependent population is biased toward services, which are nontradable goods, based on Braude (2000). An increase in their proportion in the population shifts aggregate demand in an economy from a tradable goods-oriented structure to a nontradable goods-oriented structure, which shifts aggregate supply in the same direction.[6] An economy should not produce all kinds of tradable goods consumed by themselves, because the economy can derive mutual gains from international trade by specializing in the production of limited tradable goods. Therefore, an increase in an economy's share of working-age population increases inter–industry trade based on comparative advantage or intra–industry trade based on increasing returns to scale and imperfect competition. Fukumoto and Kinugasa (2017) found that the share of working-age population in the total population has a positive effect on trade openness, using panel data of 85 countries from 1991 to 2010.[7]

Hill (1989) and Herbertsson and Zoega (1999) suggested that there exists a relationship between age structure and trade balance to GDP ratio. Their idea is based on the hypothesis that an increase in the share of working-age population improves the current account balance to GDP ratio (i.e., share of saving minus investment in GDP).[8] The trade balance is a part of the current account balance. Therefore, it is possible that age structure influences the trade balance to GDP ratio. Hill (1989) insisted that basic changes in demography are capable of producing large swings in the trade balance in the United States. In his simulations, its net exports move from a deficit of 2.2% of GNP in 1980 to a surplus of 4.4% of GNP in 2009. Herbertsson and Zoega (1999) insisted that trade deficit in the United States, Africa, and Latin America and the Caribbean and trade surplus in Japan, West-Germany, and East Asian and South-East Asian economies in the 1980 s were influenced greatly by the share of working-age population.[9]

1.3 Model and Data

We investigate whether age structure influences trade openness and trade balance to GDP ratio, incorporating several factors suggested by previous studies to influence international trade. We deal with panel data of 19 APEC economies, excluding Brunei Darussalam and Papua New Guinea, covering the period from 1951 to 2010. Brunei Darussalam is a very small country with a population less than 500,000 and depends

[6]A higher demand for nontradable goods could increase their price. Braude (2000) suggested that there exists a relationship between age structure and real exchange rate.

[7]The point of view of Tian et al. (2011) is similar to that of Fukumoto and Kinugasa (2017). Tian et al. (2011) insisted that there exists a relationship between age structure and bilateral trade, based on a gravity model in international trade with demography.

[8]For example, see Higgins (1998).

[9]The findings of Fukumoto and Kinugasa (2017) do not necessarily contradict those of Hill (1989) and Herbertsson and Zoega (1999). See Fukumoto and Kinugasa (2017, Sect. 2).

on export of energy resources such as crude oil and natural gas; thus, it will be difficult to analyze this country together with other economies. Furthermore, data for Papua New Guinea are not available. We conduct empirical analyses using two kinds of samples: 19 APEC economies; and 16 APEC economies excluding three supertrading economies—Hong Kong, Malaysia, and Singapore. In the supertrading economies, trade openness and fluctuations in trade balance to GDP ratio are extremely high. Hence, it is possible that the effects of age structure and factors other than age structure on international trade are different between supertrading economies and other APEC economies.

In the equation with trade openness as the dependent variable, the independent variables are the variables of age structure, government size, economy size, economic development, and period dummies.[10] In the equation of trade balance to GDP ratio, the independent variables are the variables of age structure, government size, export price, import price, and period dummies. We explain all the independent variables as follows:

For the variable of *Age structure*, we use two age-structure variables: (1) share of the working-age population; and (2) dependency ratio. The share of working-age population is defined as the ratio of the working-age population aged 15–64 to the total population. It is expected that the share of the working-age population has positive effects on trade openness and trade balance to GDP ratio. The dependency ratio is defined as the ratio of young dependent population aged 0–14 and old dependent population aged 65 and over to the working-age population aged 15–64. We expect that the dependency ratio has negative effects on trade openness and trade balance to GDP ratio.

Another independent variable is *Government size*. Government size is defined as the share of government consumption in GDP. Benarroch and Pandey (2008) found a negative causality from government size to trade openness. It is therefore possible that government size has a negative effect on trade openness. The empirical results of Fukumoto and Kinugasa (2017) seem to support Benarroch and Pandey (2008). In addition, the literature on the open economy macroeconomics usually suggests that fiscal expansion, involving increase of government spending and reduction of taxes, decreases trade balance regardless of a fixed or floating exchange rate regime.[11] We expect that the government size has a negative effect on trade balance to GDP ratio.

We also consider *Economy size* as a factor that affects trade openness. We use population for the variable of economy size. Alesina and Wacziarg (1998) discussed that smaller countries should trade more. We expect that the economy size has a negative effect on trade openness. The empirical results of Fukumoto and Kinugasa (2017) mostly support Alesina and Wacziarg (1998). However, some researchers are skeptical about the relationship between economy size and trade openness. For example, Krugman (1995, p. 335) pointed that the traditional link between the population of a country and its trade share is weakened by the effects of the sliced-up

[10] In the equation with trade openness, the independent variables are selected based on Fukumoto and Kinugasa (2017, Sect. 3).

[11] For example, see Feenstra and Taylor (2014, Chap. 18).

value chain in world trade. In addition, Ram (2009) reexamined the study of Alesina and Wacziarg and found that population did not necessarily have a negative effect on trade openness.

We use real GDP per capita as a measure for *Economic development*. As pointed by Feenstra (1998), it is possible that the weight of luxury service increases if an economy becomes wealthier. Therefore, real GDP per capita would have a negative effect on trade openness. Ram (2009) uses real GDP per capita as a control variable to analyze the effect of country size on trade openness.

It is expected that trade balance to GDP ratio is influenced by *Export price* and *Import price*. Usually, an increase in export price decreases the volume of exports, so that the export price has a negative effect on trade balance. Furthermore, an increase in import price decreases the volume of imports; therefore, the import price has a positive effect on trade balance.

When we set trade openness as the dependent variable, we use *Period dummies* for the variables of macroeconomic and trade policies driven by APEC, worldwide policy-led trade liberalization, transportation cost, foreign outsourcing, and global and regional economic shocks.[12] It would be difficult to include these proxy variables because of data restriction. It is possible that these effects simultaneously spread to many economies, and thus, it is reasonable that period dummy variables represent these factors.[13] In addition, we use period dummies for the variables of regional economic shocks in case the dependent variable is trade balance to GDP ratio. Trade partners of APEC economies are not limited within APEC; for example, if demand in non-APEC economies increase, trade balance will be improved in APEC economies.[14]

Our data sources are as follows: The variables for age structure are obtained from *World Population Prospects: The 2015 Revision* by the United Nations, Department of Economic and Social Affairs, Population Division for all economies except Taiwan.[15] For Taiwan, we use the data of population size from the *Human Mortality Database* for age-structure variables.[16] The data for other variables are obtained from *Penn World Table 8.0*. Trade openness is calculated as the sum of the absolute

[12]Frankel et al. (1995) point that APEC has a trade-enhancing power because the estimated coefficients of APEC dummy variables included in the gravity model are significantly positive for increases in bilateral trade volumes. However, Polak (1996) is skeptical about their findings.

[13]We do not include tariff rate in our empirical analyses because the data are available from 1951 only for few economies. However, this may not influence our empirical results significantly. Fukumoto and Kinugasa (2017) selected the data after 1991, since the data on tariff rate are available for many economies. The tariff rate has a negative effect on trade openness when only high-income countries are included in the sample (Fukumoto and Kinugasa 2017, Table 3). Ram (2009) did not include tariff rates when testing the effect of economy size on trade openness.

[14]The effects of energy prices on trade balance might be limited because some APEC economies export crude oil and others import it.

[15]File POP/15-1: Annual total population (both sexes combined) by five-year age group, major area, region and country, 1950–2100 (thousands).

[16]For Taiwan, two kinds of population size are reported in 1992: "1992−" and "1992+." Since these two do not very differ from each other, the empirical results will not be greatly influenced. We use data for "1992−" in the empirical analyses.

values of the shares of merchandise exports and imports in GDP (Indicator Codes: csh_x and csh_m, respectively).[17] Trade balance to GDP ratio is calculated as the sum of the values of the shares of merchandise exports and imports in GDP. Government size is represented by the share of government consumption in GDP (Indicator Code: csh_g). Population is expressed in millions (Indicator Code: pop). We calculated GDP per capita using the data of real GDP and population (Indicator Codes: rgdpo and pop, respectively). Export price and import price represent the price level of exports and imports, respectively (Indicator Codes: pl_x and pl_m, respectively).

We calculate the five-year average data from 1951 to 2010 and construct panel data for 12 periods: 1951–1955, 1956–1960, 1961–1965, 1966–1970, 1971–1975, 1976–1980, 1981–1985, 1986–1990, 1991–1995, 1996–2000, 2001–2005, and 2006–2010.[18] In the empirical analyses, we do not take natural logarithm of trade openness and trade balance to GDP ratio, which are dependent variables. This is because it is possible to take natural logarithm for trade openness but not for trade balance to GDP ratio.[19] Age-structure variables are natural logged in some specifications and not in others. The share of government consumption in GDP is logged when age-structure variables are natural logged, and not otherwise. Population, GDP per capita, export price, and import price are natural logged. Tables 1.1 and 1.2 present the descriptive statistics of the data used in our empirical analyses for 19 and 16 APEC economies, respectively. Table 1.1 differs significantly from Table 1.2 in terms of standard deviations of trade openness and the trade balance to GDP ratio. Standard deviations of trade openness and the trade balance to GDP ratio in Table 1.1 are much greater than those in Table 1.2. It seems that only dependent variables are influenced greatly by the inclusion of supertrading economies.

In Figs. 1.4, 1.5, 1.6, 1.7, the variables of age structure and international trade are plotted, and the results of single regression models are reported.[20] Figures 1.4 and 1.5 show the positive relationship between the share of working-age population and trade openness, which supports Fukumoto and Kinugasa (2017). In Fig. 1.5, the slopes are smaller and values of R-squared are larger than those in Fig. 1.4. Figures 1.6 and 1.7 show the positive relationship between the share of working-age population and trade balance to GDP ratio, and this is consistent with Hill (1989) and Herbertsson and Zoega (1999). In Fig. 1.7, the slopes and values of R-squared are larger than those in Fig. 1.6. Comparing the values of R-squared in Figs. 1.4 and 1.5 with Figs. 1.6 and 1.7, it seems that the effect of age structure on trade balance to GDP ratio is much smaller than that on trade openness. Moreover, the values of R-squared in Figs. 1.4 and 1.6 are much smaller than Figs. 1.5 and 1.7. It is possible

[17] For Russia, imports from 1991 to 1995 are reported as zero.

[18] If there is a missing value in any period, we do not include the period in the sample. Data for Australia, Canada, Chile, Japan, Mexico, New Zealand, Peru, the Philippines, Thailand, and the United States are available for the entire sample period. However, data for China, the Republic of Korea, and Malaysia are available from 1956–1960; for Hong Kong, Indonesia, and Singapore from 1961–1965; for Taiwan and View Nam from 1971–1975; and for Russia from 1991–1995.

[19] Fukumoto and Kinugasa (2017) took natural logarithm for trade openness.

[20] In Figs. 1.4, 1.5, 1.6, 1.7, we consider the share of working-age population as the age-structure variable, but our result is consistent even when we use dependency ratio.

Table 1.1 Descriptive statistics of variables for 19 APEC economies

Variable	Obs.	Mean	S. D.	Min	Max
Trade openness	203	0.543	0.734	0.011	4.386
Trade balance to GDP ratio	203	−0.007	0.089	−0.527	0.224
Share of the working-age population	203	0.618	0.064	0.495	0.749
Log of share of the working-age population	203	−0.487	0.106	−0.702	−0.290
Dependency ratio	203	0.636	0.175	0.336	1.018
Log of dependency ratio	203	−0.490	0.275	−1.091	0.018
Share of government consumption in GDP	203	0.151	0.050	0.034	0.322
Log of share of government consumption in GDP	203	−1.950	0.378	−3.388	−1.133
Log of population	203	3.495	1.495	0.585	7.174
Log of real GDP per capita	203	8.888	1.064	6.651	10.774
Log of export price	203	−1.019	0.668	−3.560	−0.130
Log of import price	203	−1.039	0.667	−2.595	−0.059

Table 1.2 Descriptive statistics of variables for 16 APEC economies

Variable	Obs.	Mean	S. D.	Min	Max
Trade openness	172	0.305	0.189	0.011	0.909
Trade balance to GDP ratio	172	0.001	0.046	−0.092	0.224
Share of the working-age population	172	0.615	0.062	0.495	0.738
Log of share of the working-age population	172	−0.492	0.102	−0.702	−0.304
Dependency ratio	172	0.644	0.170	0.355	1.018
Log of dependency ratio	172	−0.475	0.262	−1.035	0.018
Share of government consumption in GDP	172	0.157	0.048	0.034	0.322
Log of share of government consumption in GDP	172	−1.901	0.340	−3.388	−1.133
Log of population	172	3.795	1.393	0.712	7.174
Log of real GDP per capita	172	8.817	1.081	6.651	10.655
Log of export price	172	−1.026	0.675	−3.560	−0.130
Log of import price	172	−1.055	0.680	−2.595	−0.059

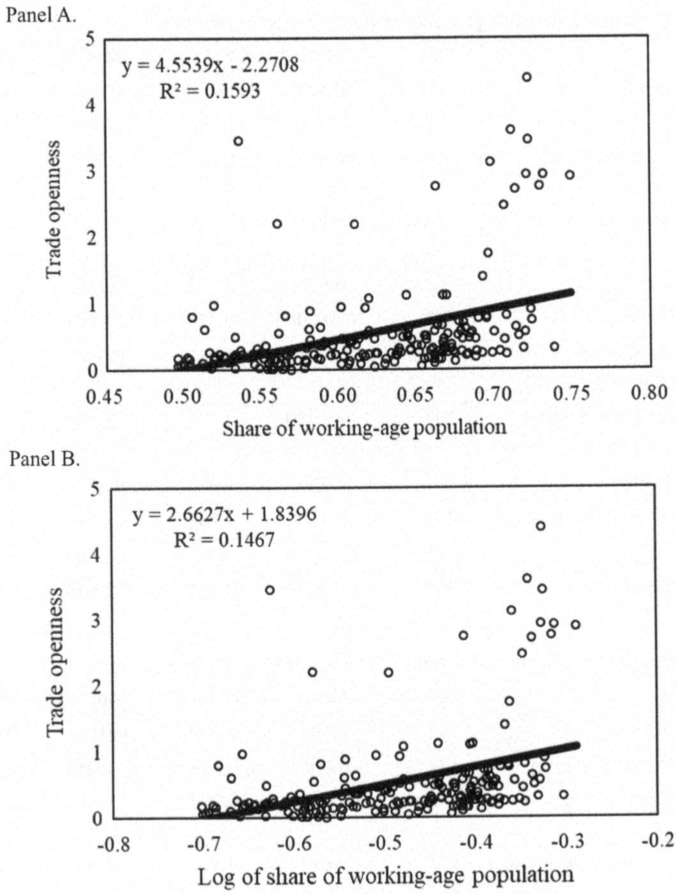

Fig. 1.4 Relationship between age structure and trade openness in 19 APEC economies. *Note* In Panel **A**, x represents the share of working-age population, and y represents the trade openness. In Panel **B**, x represents the log of share of working-age population, and y represents the trade openness. Equations in both panels are based on pooled estimation without period dummies

that the relationship between age structure and international trade in supertrading economies is different from other APEC economies, although we cannot conclude without considering other factors that influence international trade. According to Figs. 1.4, 1.5, 1.6, 1.7, our empirical results are not likely to be influenced regardless of whether logarithm is taken for the share of working-age population or not.

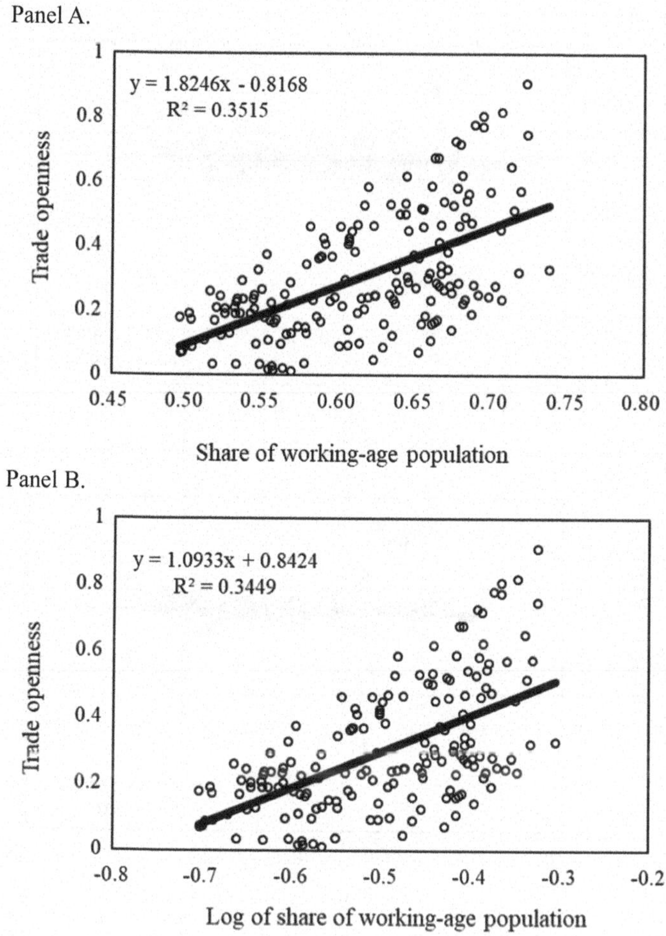

Fig. 1.5 Relationship between age structure and trade openness in 16 APEC economies. *Note* See the note of Fig. 1.4

1.4 Estimation Results

Based on the discussion in Sect. 1.3, first, we conduct empirical analyses setting the trade openness as the dependent variable and the variables of age structure, the government consumption's share of GDP, population, GDP per capita, and the period dummies as the independent variables. Then, we conduct empirical analyses setting the trade balance to GDP ratio as the dependent variable and the variables of age structure, the government consumption's share of GDP, export price, import price, and the period dummies as the independent variables. We conduct empirical analyses with two kinds of samples: (1) 19 economies with supertrading economies; and

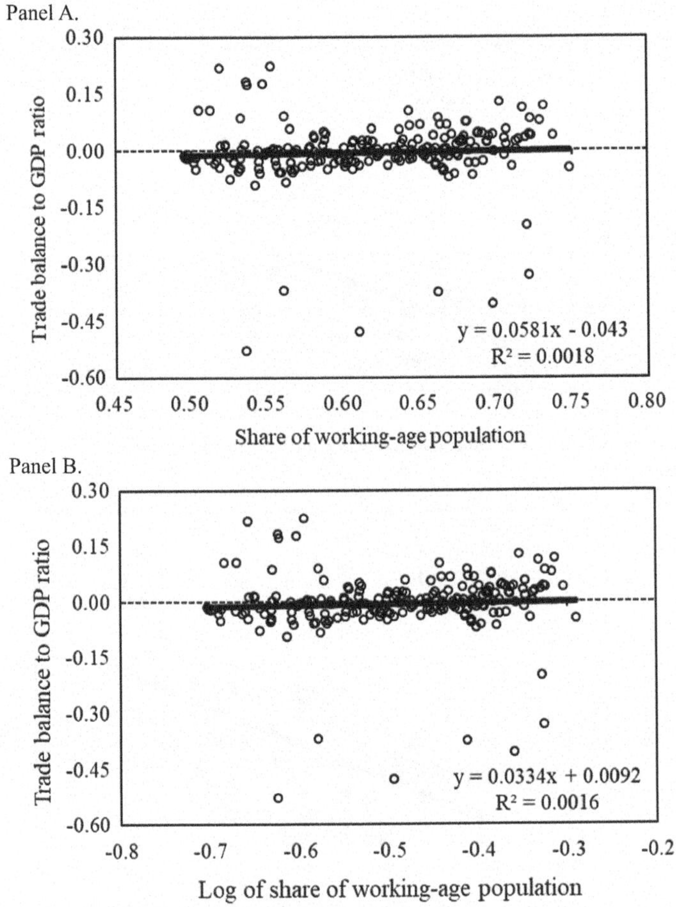

Fig. 1.6 Relationship between age structure and trade balance in 19 APEC economies. *Note* In Panel **A**, x represents the share of working-age population, and y represents the trade balance to GDP ratio. In Panel **B**, x represents the log of share of working-age population, and y represents the trade balance to GDP ratio. Equations in both panels are based on pooled estimation without period dummies

(2) 16 economies without supertrading economies. We estimate the equations including the economy dummies by using the fixed-effects model.[21]

In Tables 1.3 and 1.4, the dependent variables are trade openness. Table 1.3 presents the estimation results when 19 APEC economies are used. Coefficients of both logged and not-logged share of the working-age population are positive and

[21] Random-effects model assumes that economy fixed effects are not correlated with the independent variables. The model may not be appropriate for this study because economy fixed effects such as tradition, language, culture, and geographical conditions of each economy are likely to be correlated with independent variables.

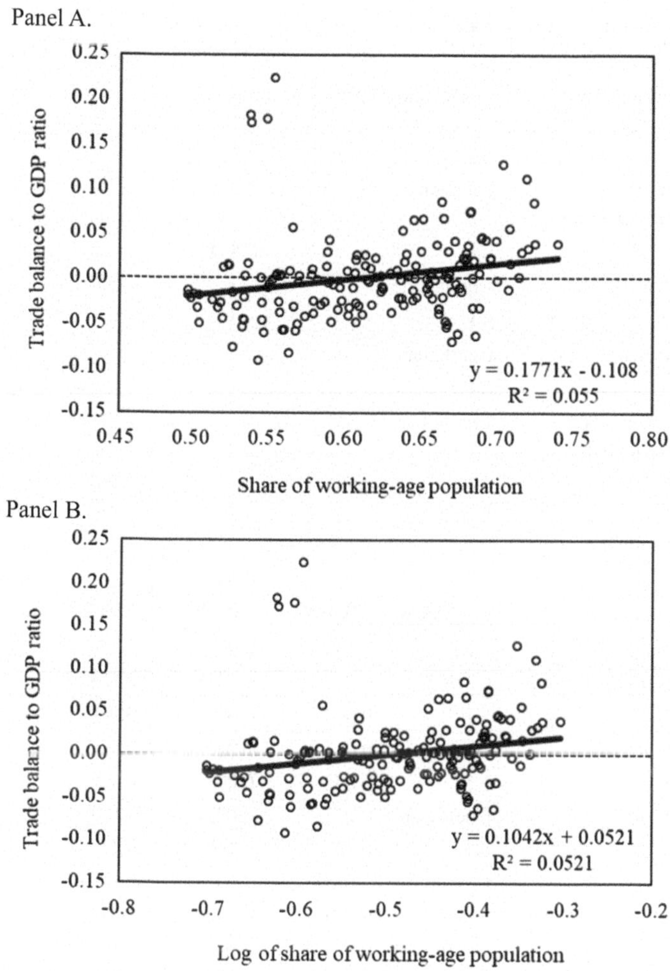

Fig. 1.7 Relationship between age structure and trade balance in 16 APEC economies. *Note* See the note of Fig. 1.6

statistically significant. The estimated coefficients of the logged dependency ratio are significantly negative. The estimated coefficient of the logged share of government consumption in GDP is significantly positive. The estimated coefficients of population are not significant. The estimated coefficients of real GDP per capita are positive and statistically significant in two estimations. Period dummies are not significant in any estimations.

Table 1.4 presents the empirical results with 16 APEC economies and is different from Table 1.3 as follows. The estimated coefficients of the dependency ratio are significantly negative for both estimations regardless of whether it is logged or not. The estimated coefficients of the share of government consumption in GDP and real

Table 1.3 Empirical results on trade openness for 19 APEC economies

		(1)	(2)	(3)	(4)
Share of working-age population	Coefficient	2.060**			
	S.E.	0.901			
Log of share of working-age population	Coefficient		0.984*		
	S.E.		0.554		
Dependency ratio	Coefficient			−0.357	
	S.E.			0.338	
Log of dependency ratio	Coefficient				−0.580***
	S.E.				0.206
Share of government consumption in GDP	Coefficient	0.331		0.302	
	S.E.	0.581		0.588	
Log of share of government consumption in GDP	Coefficient		0.136*		0.137*
	S.E.		0.080		0.079
Log of population	Coefficient	−0.075	−0.149	−0.029	−0.165
	S.E.	0.190	0.197	0.203	0.187
Log of real GDP per capita	Coefficient	0.095	0.133*	0.154**	0.079
	S.E.	0.073	0.070	0.069	0.073
1956–1960	Coefficient	0.021	0.022	0.000	0.036
	S.E.	0.098	0.098	0.100	0.096
1961–1965	Coefficient	0.022	0.022	−0.020	0.050
	S.E.	0.107	0.108	0.112	0.104
1966–1970	Coefficient	−0.090	−0.093	−0.143	−0.058
	S.E.	0.121	0.123	0.127	0.118
1971–1975	Coefficient	−0.117	−0.125	−0.173	−0.086
	S.E.	0.132	0.134	0.138	0.129
1976–1980	Coefficient	−0.095	−0.099	−0.143	−0.065
	S.E.	0.143	0.145	0.148	0.140
1981–1985	Coefficient	−0.100	−0.101	−0.137	−0.077
	S.E.	0.153	0.154	0.158	0.150
1986–1990	Coefficient	−0.148	−0.142	−0.179	−0.122
	S.E.	0.167	0.168	0.172	0.164
1991–1995	Coefficient	0.007	0.021	−0.030	0.045
	S.E.	0.185	0.186	0.190	0.182
1996–2000	Coefficient	0.015	0.038	−0.021	0.059
	S.E.	0.197	0.199	0.203	0.194
2001–2005	Coefficient	0.033	0.062	0.004	0.076
	S.E.	0.207	0.209	0.213	0.204

(continued)

Table 1.3 (continued)

2006–2010	Coefficient	0.031	0.065	0.005	0.074
	S.E.	0.220	0.222	0.226	0.216
Adjusted R-squared		0.284	0.285	0.267	0.304
Number of Observations		203	203	203	203

Note The estimates of economy dummies are not reported in our empirical results. ***, **, and * indicate significance at the 1, 5, and 10% levels, respectively

Table 1.4 Empirical results on trade openness for 16 APEC economies

		(1)	(2)	(3)	(4)
Share of working-age population	Coefficient	1.609***			
	S.E.	0.284			
Log of share of working-age population	Coefficient		1.017***		
	S.E.		0.174		
Dependency ratio	Coefficient			−0.623***	
	S.E.			0.105	
Log of dependency ratio	Coefficient				−0.368***
	S.E.				0.066
Share of government consumption in GDP	Coefficient	−0.096		−0.098	
	S.E.	0.177		0.175	
Log of share of government consumption in GDP	Coefficient		0.009		0.009
	S.E.		0.025		0.025
Log of population	Coefficient	−0.110*	−0.157**	−0.170***	−0.110*
	S.E.	0.061	0.064	0.065	0.062
Log of real GDP per capita	Coefficient	0.009	0.016	0.016	0.012
	S.E.	0.023	0.022	0.022	0.023
1956–1960	Coefficient	−0.003	0.004	0.007	−0.004
	S.E.	0.029	0.030	0.030	0.030
1961–1965	Coefficient	0.029	0.042	0.048	0.027
	S.E.	0.033	0.034	0.034	0.033
1966–1970	Coefficient	0.032	0.049	0.058	0.029
	S.E.	0.038	0.039	0.040	0.038
1971–1975	Coefficient	0.042	0.059	0.071	0.037
	S.E.	0.043	0.043	0.044	0.043
1976–1980	Coefficient	0.069	0.085*	0.098**	0.063
	S.E.	0.047	0.047	0.048	0.047
1981–1985	Coefficient	0.056	0.071	0.085*	0.049

(continued)

Table 1.4 (continued)

		(1)	(2)	(3)	(4)
	S.E.	0.050	0.050	0.051	0.050
1986–1990	Coefficient	0.016	0.033	0.047	0.010
	S.E.	0.054	0.055	0.055	0.054
1991–1995	Coefficient	0.066	0.086	0.099	0.062
	S.E.	0.060	0.060	0.061	0.060
1996–2000	Coefficient	0.116*	0.139**	0.152**	0.113*
	S.E.	0.063	0.064	0.064	0.064
2001–2005	Coefficient	0.166**	0.192***	0.206***	0.163**
	S.E.	0.067	0.067	0.068	0.067
2006–2010	Coefficient	0.222***	0.250***	0.266***	0.218***
	S.E.	0.071	0.071	0.072	0.071
Adjusted R-squared		0.727	0.730	0.732	0.724
Number of Observations		172	172	172	172

Note See the note of Table 1.3

GDP per capita are not significant in any case. All of the estimated coefficients of population are negative and statistically significant. Period dummies are significantly positive in the latter half of the 1970s and in the former half of the 1980s in some estimations, and significantly positive and gradually larger in later periods for all estimations after the latter half of the 1990s.

Values of adjusted R-squared are larger in Table 1.4 than in Table 1.3. Moreover, the deviation from the discussion of Sects. 1.2 and 1.3 seems to be smaller in Table 1.4 than in Table 1.3. According to the estimated results of Table 1.4, an increase in the share of working-age population and a decrease in the dependency ratio increase trade openness. This result is consistent with Fukumoto and Kinugasa (2017). Figures 1.1 and 1.3 show that age structure has contributed to an increase in trade openness in many APEC economies since 1970s. The estimated coefficients of the population are negative, which supports Alesina and Wacziarg (1998). The estimated results of period dummies imply that factors influencing all the APEC economies, for example, decreases in trade barriers and increases in outsourcing, have significantly contributed to increases in trade openness since the latter half of the 1990s. On the other hand, the estimated coefficients of the share of government consumption in GDP and GDP per capita are expected to be negative according to Benarroch and Pandey (2008) and Feenstra (1998), but this result is not observed in Tables 1.3 and 1.4.

In Tables 1.5 and 1.6, the dependent variables are the trade balance to GDP ratio. Table 1.5 presents the estimation results when 19 APEC economies are used. Coefficients of both logged and not-logged share of the working-age population are positive and statistically significant. The estimated coefficient of the logged dependency ratio is significantly negative. The share of government consumption in GDP are not significant in any cases. The coefficients of export price are negative in all estimations

Table 1.5 Empirical results on trade balance to GDP ratio for 19 APEC economies

		(1)	(2)	(3)	(4)
Share of working-age population	Coefficient	0.450**			
	S.E.	0.187			
Log of share of working-age population	Coefficient		0.216*		
	S.E.		0.116		
Dependency ratio	Coefficient			−0.093	
	S.E.			0.071	
Log of dependency ratio	Coefficient				−0.117***
	S.E.				0.043
Share of government consumption in GDP	Coefficient	0.066		0.038	
	S.E.	0.140		0.141	
Log of share of government consumption in GDP	Coefficient		0.009		0.012
	S.E.		0.020		0.019
Log of export price	Coefficient	−0.112***	−0.113***	−0.111***	−0.114***
	S.E.	0.024	0.025	0.024	0.024
Log of import price	Coefficient	0.093**	0.086**	0.081*	0.094**
	S.E.	0.041	0.041	0.041	0.040
1956–1960	Coefficient	0.010	0.010	0.009	0.010
	S.E.	0.024	0.025	0.025	0.024
1961–1965	Coefficient	−0.015	−0.016	−0.017	−0.015
	S.E.	0.024	0.025	0.025	0.024
1966–1970	Coefficient	−0.010	−0.010	−0.010	−0.011
	S.E.	0.027	0.027	0.027	0.027
1971–1975	Coefficient	−0.016	−0.012	−0.009	−0.017
	S.E.	0.036	0.036	0.037	0.036
1976–1980	Coefficient	−0.009	0.001	0.007	−0.010
	S.E.	0.051	0.051	0.052	0.050
1981–1985	Coefficient	−0.019	−0.006	0.004	−0.021
	S.E.	0.060	0.060	0.061	0.059
1986–1990	Coefficient	−0.001	0.015	0.027	−0.005
	S.E.	0.070	0.070	0.071	0.069
1991–1995	Coefficient	−0.025	−0.007	0.006	−0.030
	S.E.	0.074	0.074	0.075	0.073
1996–2000	Coefficient	−0.005	0.014	0.029	−0.010
	S.E.	0.076	0.076	0.077	0.075
2001–2005	Coefficient	0.004	0.024	0.040	−0.002
	S.E.	0.076	0.076	0.077	0.075

(continued)

Table 1.5 (continued)

		(1)	(2)	(3)	(4)
2006–2010	Coefficient	−0.001	0.023	0.041	−0.008
	S.E.	0.086	0.086	0.087	0.085
Adjusted R-squared		0.041	0.029	0.019	0.052
Number of observations		203	203	203	203

Note See the note of Table 1.3

Table 1.6 Empirical results on trade balance to GDP ratio for 16 APEC economies

		(1)	(2)	(3)	(4)
Share of working-age Population	Coefficient	0.266***			
	S.E.	0.090			
Log of share of Working-age population	Coefficient		0.150***		
	S.E.		0.056		
Dependency ratio	Coefficient			−0.075**	
	S.E.			0.034	
Log of dependency ratio	Coefficient				−0.068***
	S.E.				0.021
Share of government consumption in GDP	Coefficient	−0.171***		−0.185***	
	S.E.	0.064		0.064	
Log of share of government consumption in GDP	Coefficient		−0.021**		−0.019**
	S.E.		0.009		0.009
Log of export price	Coefficient	−0.093***	−0.092***	−0.093***	−0.093***
	S.E.	0.011	0.011	0.011	0.011
Log of import price	Coefficient	0.102***	0.106***	0.099***	0.108***
	S.E.	0.018	0.018	0.018	0.018
1956–1960	Coefficient	−0.008	−0.008	−0.008	−0.008
	S.E.	0.011	0.011	0.011	0.011
1961–1965	Coefficient	−0.006	−0.006	−0.006	−0.006
	S.E.	0.011	0.011	0.011	0.011
1966–1970	Coefficient	−0.020*	−0.020*	−0.019	−0.021*
	S.E.	0.012	0.012	0.012	0.012
1971–1975	Coefficient	−0.021	−0.024	−0.018	−0.025
	S.E.	0.016	0.016	0.016	0.016
1976–1980	Coefficient	−0.021	−0.026	−0.017	−0.029
	S.E.	0.022	0.023	0.023	0.022
1981–1985	Coefficient	−0.025	−0.032	−0.019	−0.035

(continued)

Table 1.6 (continued)

		(1)	(2)	(3)	(4)
	S.E.	0.026	0.027	0.027	0.026
1986–1990	Coefficient	−0.027	−0.034	−0.019	−0.039
	S.E.	0.031	0.031	0.031	0.031
1991–1995	Coefficient	−0.046	−0.053	−0.038	−0.058*
	S.E.	0.033	0.033	0.033	0.033
1996–2000	Coefficient	−0.045	−0.051	−0.035	−0.057*
	S.E.	0.033	0.034	0.034	0.033
2001–2005	Coefficient	−0.044	−0.049	−0.033	−0.056*
	S.E.	0.034	0.034	0.034	0.034
2006–2010	Coefficient	−0.049	−0.055	−0.036	−0.063
	S.E.	0.038	0.039	0.039	0.038
Adjusted R−squared		0.363	0.343	0.346	0.359
Number of Observations		172	172	172	172

Note See the note of Table 1.3

and significant, and all of the estimated effects of import price are positive and significant. Period dummies are not significant in any estimations.

Table 1.6 presents the empirical results with 16 APEC economies. This table is different from Table 1.5 in the following ways. The estimated coefficients of the dependency ratio are significantly negative for both estimations regardless of whether it is logged or not. All of the estimated coefficients of the share of government consumption in GDP are negative and statistically significant. Coefficients of some period dummies are significantly negative in three estimated equations.

Values of adjusted R-squared in Table 1.6 are greater than those in Table 1.5. Moreover, the results in Table 1.6 are almost consistent with the discussion in Sects. 1.2 and 1.3. Not only Tables 1.3 and 1.4 but also Tables 1.5 and 1.6 suggest that conducting empirical analyses on international trade including both supertrading economies and other APEC economics may lead to incorrect conclusions. According to the estimated results of Table 1.6, an increase in the share of working-age population and a decrease in dependency ratio increase the trade surplus to GDP ratio. This result supports Hill (1989) and Herbertsson and Zoega (1999). Inferring from Figs. 1.2 and 1.3, it is plausible that a rapid increase in the share of working-age population in many Asian economies improved their trade balance and worsened the trade balance in the trade partner, the United States. However, it should be noted that the effect of age structure on trade balance to GDP ratio is much smaller than the effect of age structure on trade openness with reference to Tables 1.4 and 1.6. That is, factors other than age structure must greatly influence the trade balance to GDP ratio. An increase in the share of government consumption in GDP has worsened trade balance. These results could be consistent with orthodox open economy macroeconomics. In all estimations of Tables 1.5 and 1.6, the coefficients of export and import prices are significantly negative and positive, respectively. Therefore, decreasing global trade imbalance would be possible to some extent by shrinking the government size of the United States and keeping an increase in export price in the United States lower than Asian economies.[22] In Table 1.6, period dummies are significant at only 10% level. Comparing this with Table 1.4, the effects of period dummies on trade balance to GDP ratio seem to be much smaller than those on trade openness.

1.5 Conclusions

In this study, we attempted to clarify whether age structure influences trade openness and trade balance to GDP ratio in APEC economies. From the empirical results of 16 APEC economies, we found that the share of working-age population has significantly positive effects on trade openness and trade balance to GDP ratio, and that dependency ratio has significantly negative effects on them. Our empirical results are consistent with the hypotheses of Fukumoto and Kinugasa (2017), Hill (1989), and Herbertsson and Zoega (1999). The share of working-age population is increasing in many APEC economies; in particular, it is increasing at a rapid pace in many Asian economies. Age structure has contributed to an increase in trade openness in APEC economies, and the chronic trade surplus with the United States in Asian economies could be explained by a rapid demographic change in Asian economies to some extent. Of course, we should not overstress the effect of age structure on international trade. As is inferred from the positive effects of period dummies on trade openness, boosts in trade openness since the 1990 s are not caused solely by demographic changes. Moreover, our empirical results show that the share of government consumption in GDP, export price, and import price influence trade balance to GDP ratio.

We also conducted empirical analyses with 19 APEC economies, by including three supertrading economies: Hong Kong, Malaysia, and Singapore. Regarding the effects of not only age structure but also factors other than age structure on international trade, the empirical results with the 19 APEC economies deviated more from Fukumoto and Kinugasa (2017), Hill (1989), and Herbertsson and Zoega (1999) than those with 16 APEC economies. Trade structures in supertrading economies seemed to be different from other APEC economies. The link between the demography of an economy and its international trade might be weakened in trade-oriented economies.

In the future, demographic change may affect trade openness and trade balance to GDP ratio in APEC economies inversely from the past. Low fertility and population aging in Asian economies, which has a large share of population in APEC

[22] It is not perfectly deniable that Asian economies made their own currency cheaper in order to decrease export price and increase import price, but this would not be the main reason of chronic trade imbalance. As a matter of fact, it is unrealistic that the United States has approved the control of nominal exchange rate by Asian economies for decades. In addition, it would be difficult for Asian economies to control real exchange rate through nominal exchange rate in the long run in order to maintain their price competitiveness.

economies, will accelerate. Children born in times of low fertility would become part of the working-age generation 15 years later. Moreover, the share of old-dependent population is expected to increase rapidly because of longer life expectancy. These indicate that the share of the working-age population will decrease a few decades later. Therefore, the demography in Asian economies could slow down increases in trade openness and trade balance to GDP ratio, and trade conflict between the United States and Asian economies might be mitigated.

Acknowledgements This research was started when we were visiting scholars at the East-West Center in Honolulu, Hawaii from August 2013 to August 2014. During this period, we benefited from discussions with Professor Andrew Mason on population economics. In addition, we appreciate the valuable comments of Professors Mitoshi Yamaguchi, Ryuzo Miyao, Yun Zhang, Toshiki Jinushi, Serena Rhee, Hiroko Hagiwara, and Masahiko Shibamoto. This work was supported by JSPS KAKENHI Grant Numbers JP26292118 and JP24310031 and Program to Supporting Research Activities of Female Researchers (Collaborations) funded within support the Development of Human Resources in Science and Technology in FY2014 by MEXT.

References

Alesina A, Wacziarg R (1998) Openness, country size and government. J Public Econ 69:305–321

Benarroch M, Pandey M (2008) Trade openness and government size. Econ Lett 101:157–159

Braude J (2000) Age structure and the real exchange rate. Bank Isr Discuss Pap Ser 2000:10

Dooley MP, Folkerts-Landau D, Garber P (2004) The revived Bretton Woods system. Int J Financ Econ 9:307–313

Feenstra RC (1998) Integration of trade and disintegration of production in the global economy. J Econ Perspect 12:31–50

Feenstra RC, Taylor AM (2014) International economics, 3rd edn. Worth Publishers, New York

Frankel JA, Wei SJ, Stein E (1995) APEC and regional trading arrangements in the Pacific. In: Dobson W, Flatters F (eds) Pacific trade and investment: options for the 1990s. Kingston, Canada, John Deutsch Institute, pp 289–312

Fukumoto Y, Kinugasa T (2017) Age structure and trade openness: an empirical investigation. World Econ 40:1247–1263

Herbertsson TT, Zoega G (1999) Trade surpluses and life cycle saving behavior. Econ Lett 65:227–237

Higgins M (1998) Demography, national savings, and international capital flows. Int Econ Rev 39:343–369

Hill, J. K. (1989) Demographics and the trade balance, Economic Review (Federal Reserve Bank of Dallas), September, 1–11

Krugman P (1995) Growing world trade: causes and consequences. Brook Pap Econ Act 1:327–377

Modigliani F, Brumberg R (1954) Utility analysis and the consumption function: an interpretation of cross-section data. In: Kurihara K (ed) Post-Keynesian Economics. Rutgers University Press, New Brunswick, NJ, pp 388–436

Polak JJ (1996) Is APEC a natural regional trading bloc? A critique of the 'gravity model' of international trade. World Econ 19:533–544

Ram R (2009) Openness, country size, and government size: additional evidence from a large cross-country panel. J Public Econ 93:213–218

Tian W, Yao Y, Yu M, Zhou Y (2011) Dependency ratio and international trade. Available at SSRN 1792564

Chapter 2
Misallocation of Agglomeration Economies and Diseconomies: Evidence from China

Hongzhong Fan and Linhui Yu

Abstract Through regression analysis of a survey data collected from peasant workers in China, it is revealed that nominal wages and living costs of peasant workers are essentially identical across cities of different sizes. This finding suggests that in developing countries with conspicuous and sustained employment pressures like China, the bargaining power of low-skilled workers are so weak that they have no leverage in transferring the high costs of living in large cities to their employers by demanding better nominal wages. As a result, firms in large cities enjoy most of the benefits afforded by agglomeration at disproportionately reduced costs. In contrast, low-skilled workers bear the costs of agglomeration without earning an equitable level of benefits from living in large cities. In this case, the market mechanism that normally operates to limit city size growth evidently fails to work, which unavoidably promotes the overexpansion of megacities.

Keywords Agglomeration economies · Diseconomies · Misallocation Megacity

2.1 Introduction

As a consequence of rapid economic growth and accelerated urbanization of China in recent decades, a number of megacities have sprung up in China. According to China's sixth nationwide census (2010), the population of Beijing, Shanghai and Chongqing have already exceeded 20 million, and the population of Guangzhou, Shenzhen and Tianjin have reached 10 million (NBS 2011a). Despite prohibitive house prices in these megacities in China (E.g., house price to income ratio in Beijing was 25 in 2010), the population of these cities are poised to rise yet further. For example, during 2005–2009, the population of Beijing increased by 453,000, 430,000, 520,000, 620,000, and 600,000, on a year-on-year basis. In other words, such annual increase in Beijing's population was equivalent to the total population of a medium-sized city (BMSB 2010). It is indeed puzzling that why record-high house prices in China's megacities fail to dampen the population's impetus to climb. In this paper, we propose a theory to dissect this puzzle. The thrust of this theory is that there exists misallocation of agglomeration economies and agglomeration

T. Kinugasa et al., *Economic Growth and Transition of Industrial Structure in East Asia*, Kobe University Social Science Research Series,
https://doi.org/10.1007/978-981-13-2868-8_2

diseconomies between firms and workers in China's large cities, which undermines the market function of agglomeration diseconomies to limit city size.

Few studies so far have characterized the patterns of the allocation of agglomeration economies and agglomeration diseconomies between firms and workers, and the previous research only assumes implicitly that they impact on firms and workers to a similar extent, which may not be always the case.[1]

From the micro-foundations of urban externalities, that the concentration of economic activities has the following advantages: information spillovers about technology, suppliers, purchasers, and market conditions (Fujita and Ogawa 1982); the scope for local intra-industry specialization of plants in specific activities (Becker and Henderson 2000); increased diversity of local suppliers to local export producers (Dixit and Stigliz 1977; Abdel-Rahman and Fujita 1990); and search for matching improvements between workers and firms in local labor markets (Helsley and Strange 1990). In addition, the proximity of buyers and sellers reduces transportation costs (Krugman 1991) as well as search-related retail costs (Caplin and Leahy 1998) (see Henderson (2002) for a review).

While firms benefit from agglomerating in cities, workers in larger cities generally need to tolerate higher costs of living, much longer commuting time, crowdedness, noise, pollution and so on (Muth 1969; Fujita and Ogawa 1982). For example, in the United States and Latin American countries, the cost of living in large cities is over two times higher than that in small cities (Thomas 1980; Henderson 1988), while costs of living in Paris are 89–94% higher than that in other regions of France (Rousseau 1995). To illustrate further, the marginal investment cost (including public facilities, public services and housing) of absorbing an extra family in average urban areas of Bangladesh, Egypt, Indonesia, and Pakistan is three times higher than that in rural areas (Henderson 2002). Additionally, Zheng (2001) found that agglomeration diseconomies in Tokyo metropolitan are mainly represented by excessively high house prices, long commuting time and compromised environmental quality.

To summarize, agglomeration economies mainly confers increased productivity on firms, while agglomeration diseconomies mainly generates increased burden on workers in terms of living costs. Firms are the primary direct beneficiaries of agglomeration economies, while workers are the primary direct victims of agglomeration diseconomies. Under the condition that workers have enough bargaining power, workers in large cities can negotiate a higher salary (or nominal wage) to compensate for their higher living costs. Alternatively, they can choose to migrate to small- and medium-sized cities. In this way, the higher living costs of workers in large cities are passed on to firms, and transformed into investment costs of the firms. This cost transfer from workers to firms has very important market function, i.e., it allocates agglomeration diseconomies to firms, which effectively prevents overconcentration of firms and investors in large cities. It is this tension between economies and diseconomies that allows cities to grow without becoming too large. Therefore, the

[1]Literature featuring this postulate include Henderson (1974), Helsley and Strange (1990), Black and Henderson (1999), Fujita et al. (1999), Duranton and Puga (2001), and Au and Henderson (2006a, b).

effective city size reflects a trade-off between the higher production efficiency and the increased living costs produced by agglomeration of production and population (Davis and Henderson 2003).

It is noteworthy that, there is an important precondition for smooth transfer of the high living costs of workers in large cities into the investment costs of firms, namely: workers have enough bargaining power in wage negotiation, which requires full employment or quasi-full employment or sufficient employment insurances in the labor market. If this precondition holds, workers can negotiate a higher wage that fully or almost fully covers the costs of living in large cities. This precondition is basically valid for developed countries like the US, even when a certain degree of unemployment persists.[2] The year 2000 U.S. census revealed that the nominal wages of American workers in large metropolitan areas (i.e., with a population larger than 1.5 million people) are 32% higher than that in rural areas and small cities (i.e., with a population of less than 250,000). However, if the nominal wages are adjusted according to the local cost-of-living index and then compared in the form of "real" wages, then the real wages of workers in large metropolitan areas are not significantly different from those in rural areas and small cities (Baum-Snow and Pavan 2011). This suggests that it is possible for workers in large urban areas to successfully pass on the higher cost of living to firms by negotiation on nominal wages, thus increasing firm investment costs without a concomitant increase in the real wages of employees. This fact effectively prevents the excessive concentration of population and production in megacities.

However, for developing countries like China, the above precondition is rarely satisfied.[3] In China, for example, the employment landscape is much characterized by surplus labor in rural areas and an abundant supply of low-skilled workers residing in the cities. The bargaining power of these low-skilled workers is quite weak when compared to that of their high-skilled counterparts. To get or retain a job in a city, many low-skilled workers are willing to accept high housing costs, congested traffic, and poor environmental conditions. Many are even willing to live in slum areas and receive subsistence-level wages barely sufficient for their survival (Lewis 1954). As living in slums requires minimal housing costs, big-city firms can easily recruit enough low-skilled workers without paying an equitable level of wages to justify the costs of decent housing and living. Therefore, it is likely the case that the nominal wages of low-skilled workers in large cities may not be significantly different from those in small cities in developing countries like China. Under such circumstances, the agglomeration diseconomies which mainly lie in the higher costs of living in large cities fail to be transformed into firms' higher investment costs while firms enjoy the benefits from agglomeration economies, thus thwarting the market mechanism that otherwise prevents a developed city from overgrowing.

---

[2]On the one hand, the unemployment rate in developed countries is much lower than that in developing countries like China. On the other hand, employee unions are more powerful in developed countries, which ensure that the interests of workers are represented.

[3]This precondition was also not satisfied during the rapid urbanization of countries like Japan, Korea, and Brazil after World War II.

Compared with low-skilled workers, high-skilled workers have stronger bargaining power and earn higher wages, so they care more about house prices and living costs in large cities. However, firms tend to locate in large cities, which means large cities have more job opportunities than small cities. Over agglomeration of capital and labor in large cities will to some extent deter the mobility of high-skilled workers across cities. As a result, except for a small proportion of very-high-skilled workers who have very strong bargaining power in the labor market, most high-skilled workers are only partially compensated for the costs of decent housing and living in large cities, which further undermines the market mechanism governing urban growth.

To highlight, in countries with heavy employment pressures and insufficient unemployment insurances, firms receive a large share of the benefits of agglomeration without paying a justifiable level of operation costs. In contrast, workers bear most of the costs of agglomeration but benefit little from living in large cities.[4] This phenomenon is herein referred to as the misallocation of agglomeration economies and diseconomies between firms and workers.

There are possibly other reasons why the nominal wages of low-skill workers in large cities are not necessarily higher than those in medium and small cities. First, city amenities bears an important influence on population flows (Roback 1982). Large cities usually offer much better public services than medium and small-sized cities, and this helps to convince young, low-skill workers to accept meager wages and work for several years in large cities before returning home. Second, the study by Lucas (2004) found that low-skill workers expect faster accumulation of human capital and wages in large cities over the long term. In terms of income over the whole life cycle, young low-skill workers would rather receive relatively low real wages in large cities than work in medium and small cities. With the bargaining power of low-skill workers thus weakened, the usual function of housing prices and traffic costs in regulating the flow of low-skill workers fails to work, aggravating the misallocation of agglomeration economies and diseconomies.

One implicit assumption made in existing literature is that agglomeration economies and agglomeration diseconomies equally (or similarly) impact employers and employees. This generally holds true for developed economies like the U.S., but not necessarily in developing countries like China for the reasons described above. The existence of misallocation of agglomeration economies and agglomeration diseconomies between firms and workers undermines the market mechanisms governing city growth. As a result, firms are biased toward continuously investing and creating new jobs in large cities, and hordes of low-skilled workers who are urgently in need of jobs flood in without ambition to realize their basic concerns over housing prices and other living costs. This phenomenon causes the over-expansion of large megacities.

A possible approach to empirically demonstrate the misallocation proposed by us is to examine the relationship between city size and nominal wages as well as

---

[4]Low-skill workers also bear the costs of agglomeration diseconomies. For example, they have to live in humble rooms and bear poor environmental and traffic conditions instead of living in respectable houses. They accept slum life because they cannot afford better conditions.

living costs of low-skilled workers. China is a good example for conducting such research since it is the world's largest developing country and has huge reservoirs of low-skilled workers seeking jobs in urban growth centers. By using survey data collected in China, this paper attempted to investigate whether city size influences the nominal wages and living costs (housing costs and non-housing living costs) of low-skilled workers. The main conclusions of this paper are:

(1) Nominal wages and living costs of low-skilled workers are almost the same across cities after controlling for various factors including city amenities and vocation attributes.

(2) There exists misallocation of agglomeration economies and diseconomies between firms and workers in China, and this phenomenon is possibly generalizable to other developing countries.

(3) Such misallocation undermines the market mechanism in which factors like house prices and non-housing living costs normally plays important roles in limiting city size.

To our best knowledge, this is the first paper discussing the allocation of agglomeration economies and diseconomies between firms and workers. The main contributions of this paper lie in that: (1) It challenges the conventional assumption that agglomeration economies and agglomeration diseconomies equally impact firms and workers; (2) we provide empirical evidence that misallocation of agglomeration economies and diseconomies exists in developing countries like China; (3) we generate a new perspective that can account for over-expansion of megacities.

The rest of this paper is organized as follows: Sect. 2.2 introduces how to measure misallocation of agglomeration economies and diseconomies; Sect. 2.3 introduces the wage formation mechanism of low-skilled workers in China; Sect. 2.4 describes the data and variables; Sect. 2.5 discusses the empirical results; Sect. 2.6 is robustness checks; and Sect. 2.7 is the concluding remarks and policy suggestions.

2.2 Measuring Misallocation of Agglomeration Economies and Diseconomies

The relationship between workers' nominal wages and living costs in large cities will be analyzed in order to identify the measure of misallocation of agglomeration economies and diseconomies.

2.2.1 Living Costs and City Sizes

It is important to clearly identify two types of living costs associated with cities. The first type is the expense of having a decent living standard, denoted as C_d. The second type is the subsistence cost of living in slum areas, denoted as C_p. The subsistence costs of living in slums across different sized cities are approximately the same, which means that the living cost in slum (C_p) is irrelevant to the size of the city. However, the cost of decent living increases with the size of the city and housing prices.

2.2.2 *Nominal Wages and Decent Living Costs*

The relationship between the cost of decent living (C_d) and the nominal wage of a worker having enough bargaining power to engage in wage negotiation is considered first. For example, assume that a country has a city named "L" (a metropolis) and a city named "S" (a small city). The consumption behavior of a typical worker in city L can be represented by the following:

$$Max: U_L = G_{Lt}^{\alpha} G_{Ln}^{\beta} \tag{2.1}$$

$$S.T.\ W^L = P_{Lt} G_{Lt} + P_{Ln} G_{Ln}$$

Variable U_L represents the utility of a typical worker in city L who consumes two sets of goods and services. One is the combination of spatially tradable goods and services or G_{Ln}. The other is the combination of spatially non-tradable goods and services or G_{Lt}. P_{Lt} and P_{Ln} are the prices of the two sets of goods and services, respectively. W^L is the nominal wage of a typical worker in city L. Both α and β are positive numbers, but less than 1.

The indirect utility function of a typical worker in city L can be expressed by Eq. (2.2) after constructing a Lagrangian function to solve the foregoing optimization problem:

$$U_L = (\frac{\alpha}{\alpha+\beta})^{\alpha} \cdot (\frac{\beta}{\alpha+\beta})^{\beta} \cdot (\frac{W^L}{P_{Lt}})^{\alpha} \cdot (\frac{W^L}{P_{Ln}})^{\beta} \tag{2.2}$$

According to Eq. (2.2), the equilibrium condition of the typical worker moving between city L and city S is:

$$(\frac{W^L}{P_{Lt}})^{\alpha} \cdot (\frac{W^L}{P_{Ln}})^{\beta} = (\frac{W^S}{P_{St}})^{\alpha} \cdot (\frac{W^S}{P_{Sn}})^{\beta} \tag{2.3}$$

where W^S is the nominal wage of a typical worker in city S. P_{St} and P_{Sn} are the prices of the two sets of tradable and non-tradable goods in city S, respectively.

After applying the logarithm for both sides of the equation, the equilibrium condition for the flows of workers between large cities and small cities are as follows:

$$LnW^L - LnW^S = LnC_d^L - LnC_d^S \tag{2.4}$$

where $LnC_d^L = \alpha LnP_{Lt} + \beta LnP_{Ln}$; $LnC_d^S = \alpha LnP_{St} + \beta LnP_{Sn}$, and assuming $\alpha + \beta = 1$. C_d^L and C_d^S represent the cost of decent living in large and small cities, respectively. Equation (2.4) illustrates that where a small city is used as the benchmark, a worker possessing wage bargaining power will possess a linear relationship between his nominal wage and decent living cost. Assuming that the prices of tradable goods in both small and large cities are equal and housing is the only non-tradable good, the difference between nominal wages in small and large cities will depend on the difference between housing costs.

2.2.3 City Amenities, Workers' Bargaining Powers over Wages and Misallocation

If the effects of city amenities on worker flows are also considered, then Eq. (2.1) can be transformed into Eq. (2.5):

$$Max : U_L = A_{mL} G_{Lt}^{\alpha} G_{Ln}^{\beta} \tag{2.5}$$

$$S.T.\ W^L = P_{Lt} G_{Lt} + P_{Ln} G_{Ln}$$

where A_{mL} represents the environmental amenities in city L, and other variables are as defined in Eq. (2.1).

After optimization, the equilibrium condition of flows of representative workers across large cities and small cities is:

$$(LnW^L - LnC_d^L) + LnA_{mL} = (LnW^S - LnC_d^S) + LnA_{mS} \tag{2.6}$$

Equation (2.6) shows that the better the supply of city amenities, the lower the nominal wages $(LnW - LnC)$. That is to say, a city with a better supply of amenities enables local companies to enjoy the benefits of agglomeration economies without completely bearing the cost of diseconomies; i.e., there is no need to compensate the workers for the higher costs of decent living in larger cities. Through reducing workers' bargaining powers over wages, a better supply of city amenities operates as a driving force of misallocation of agglomeration economies and diseconomies.

2.2.4 Nominal Wages and Living Costs Under Employment Pressure

In a harsh job market, we assume that the bargaining powers of high-skill workers are not affected, while the bargaining powers of the low-skill workers are largely reduced. To survive, workers in large cities choose to accept a survival wage and live in slum-like conditions. Under these circumstances, the mobility equilibrium condition of low-skill workers from large cities to small cities, regardless of city amenities, is illustrated by Eq. (2.7):

$$LnW_p^L - LnW_p^S = LnC_p^L - LnC_p^S \approx 0 \tag{2.7}$$

where W_p^L and W_p^S represent the nominal wage of low-skill workers in large and small cities, respectively. Equation (2.7) shows that the nominal wages of low-skill workers are not related to decent living cost or city size in harsh job market periods.

In a harsh job market, if low-skill workers care about city amenities and it is assumed that large cities feature better amenities, then the nominal wages of low-skill workers in large cities are even lower when compared to their small city counterparts. Although the possibility of this is low, it does occur in the young generation of low-skill workers in China. The young generation from China's rural areas has a strong desire to live in cities, where they hope to accumulate more human capital or receive better payment. They may be temporarily supported by their parents, which allows them to accept lower wages while getting on their feet in a large city. However, low-skill workers who are older or married are unlikely to be sponsored by their parents. Therefore, this factor is considered by controlling the age of workers in the empirical analysis.

2.2.5 *Pressure of Migration and Firms' Profits in Large or Small Cities*

Assuming housing is not considered by workers, Krugman (1991) finds that under the condition that there exists economy of agglomeration and transportation cost is relatively low, all industries and population would continuously agglomerate into large cities. While Helpman (1997) finds that when housing is considered, the allocation of industries between large cities and small cities would achieve an equilibrium with the increase of workers' preference to housing, which is in contrast to Krugman (1991).

As mentioned before, bargaining power of Chinese low-skilled workers is considerably low. As a result, they receive no higher nominal wages in large cities than in small cities. In this case, low-skilled workers in large cities would care less about housing condition because of higher housing costs in large cities than in small cities. On the contrary, high-skilled workers have higher bargaining powers than low-skilled workers, so they would consider the cost of decent housing before migrating to large cities. Basing on Krugman (1991) and Helpman (1997), we analyze the migration pressure of low-skilled labor in developing countries like China.

Assume there are a large number of low-skilled labors and a small number of high-skilled labors in a developing economy, and low-skilled labors face heavy employment pressure and have low bargaining power on wage. We first assume that a typical firm only employs high-skilled workers, and its profit functions in a large city and a small city are represented in (2.8) and (2.9), respectively.

$$\pi_L = \theta_L f(L_d) - W_d^L L_d \tag{2.8}$$

$$\pi_S = \theta_S f(L_d) - W_d^S L_d \tag{2.9}$$

π_L and π_S denote the firm's profit in a large city L and a small city S, respectively. θ_L and θ_S denote the extent of economies of agglomeration enjoyed by the firm in the large city and the small city ($\theta_L > \theta_S$). L_d denotes the number of high-skilled workers employed by the firm. W_d^L and W_d^S are nominal wages of high-skilled workers in the large city and the small city ($W_d^L > W_d^S$). According to Helpman (1997), firms that only hire high-skilled workers would reach an equilibrium between the large city and the small city, and we assume the equilibrium population of the large city is N_0.

In another case, we assume that a typical firm only hires low-skilled workers, and its profit functions in a large city and a small city are represented in (2.10) and (2.11), respectively.

$$\pi_L^{'} = \theta_L f(L_p) - W_p^L L_p \tag{2.10}$$

$$\pi_S^{'} = \theta_S f(L_p) - W_p^S L_p \tag{2.11}$$

L_p denotes the number of low-skilled workers employed by the firm, W_p^L and W_p^S are the nominal wage of low-skilled workers in a large city and a small city ($W_p^L = W_p^S$). As $\theta_L > \theta_S$, when transportation cost is low, firms will continuously invest in large cities, which brings out huge migration pressure for the low-skilled labors living in small and medium cities and rural areas. To make a living or find a job, low-skilled workers prefer to work in large cities and mostly live in the city slums. Under this condition, firms in large cities enjoy the benefits of agglomeration economy without undertaking the costs of agglomeration diseconomies, which causes misallocation of agglomeration economies and diseconomies between firms and workers. Thus, destructive factors such as high house price, produced by agglomeration diseconomics, fail to work to limit the city size from overexpansion

Note that in a competitive market, firms' profits in big cities equal zero, while their profits are even below zero in small cities.

Finally, we assume that a typical firm hires both high-skilled workers and low-skilled workers, the proportion of high-skilled workers is ρ and the proportion of low-skill workers is $(1 - \rho)$. The firm will reach an equilibrium in locating in a large city or a small city according to Helpman (1997)—except that the population of the large city will be larger than N_0. Therefore, there exists partial misallocation of agglomeration economies and diseconomies, and also exists partial malfunction of agglomeration diseconomies in limiting city size in terms of destructive factors like high house price. Industries with high transportation costs such as services industries, will eventually reach an equilibrium in allocation of between large cities and small cities.

2.2.6 Complete Misallocation of Agglomeration Economies and Diseconomies

Two extreme situations are considered to measure the misallocation of agglomeration economies and diseconomies. The first is the complete misallocation of agglomeration economies and diseconomies; and the second is the complete absence of misallocation of agglomeration economies and diseconomies.

According to Eqs. (2.4) and (2.7), the complete misallocation of agglomeration economies and diseconomies is defined as when companies in large cities fully enjoy the benefits from the agglomeration economies but do not compensate low-skill workers with decent living wages. This can be illustrated by Eq. (2.12).

$$LnW_p^L - LnW_p^S \leq LnC_p^L - LnC_p^S \approx 0 \ll LnC_d^L - LnC_d^S \tag{2.12}$$

Equation (2.12) has two meanings:

(1) Except for the impact of city amenities, the nominal wages of low-skill workers have nothing to do with city size.

(2) Under the condition of high employment pressure, and where low-skill workers care more about city amenities, the nominal wages of low-skill workers can be negatively correlated to city size as big cities offer better amenities and higher wages.

Note that the definition of misallocation of agglomeration is based on low-skill workers, because high-skill workers have more bargaining power on wages and thus can ask for sufficient or at least partial payment to compensate them for the cost of decent city living.

2.2.7 No Misallocation of Agglomeration Economies and Diseconomies

No misallocation of agglomeration economies and diseconomies occurs when low-skill workers also have strong wage bargaining powers (due to unions, full employment, or an unemployment safety net, etc.). Companies must compensate low-skill workers according to decent living costs in order to keep employees, which means that companies and workers will both enjoy the benefits of agglomeration economies as well as the cost of agglomeration diseconomies. This is displayed in Eq. (2.13):

$$LnW_p^L - LnW_p^S = LnC_d^L - LnC_d^S \gg 0 \tag{2.13}$$

The equation shows that when there is no misallocation of agglomeration of economies and diseconomies, the nominal wages of low-skill workers are positively correlated with city size.

2.2.8 *Measuring Degree of Misallocation of Agglomeration Economics and Diseconomies*

The index of *MOA* (Misallocation of Agglomeration economies/diseconomies) is shown below:

$$MOA = (LnW_p^L - LnW_p^S)/(LnC_d^L - LnC_d^S) \quad (2.14)$$

Equation (2.14) demonstrates that the extent of agglomeration economies and diseconomies can be measured by the ratio of wage difference and decent living cost difference of low-skill workers between a large city and a small city. If $MOA \leq 0$, it means that full misallocation of agglomeration economies and diseconomies exists. If $MOA = 1$, it means that there is no misallocation at all. The smaller the *MOA*, the higher the extent of misallocation of agglomeration economies and diseconomies.

2.3 Peasant Workers and Wages Formation of Low-Skilled Workers in China

2.3.1 *Particularity of China's Labor Markets*

Labour forces in China's cities can be broadly divided into three categories: peasant workers, urban low-skilled workers, and high-skilled workers. Peasant workers refer to rural-to-urban migrants who hold an agricultural *hukou* (official identity of agricultural/urban residents) but work full time in cities. They mostly engage in low-wage physical or menial work in cities and reside in places of poor living conditions, e.g., in proximities of construction sites, collective dormitories, or urban slums. According to the latest statistics (NBS 2012), there are around 250 million peasant workers in China, which accounts for half of the total employment of secondary and tertiary industries in China. Among them, 156 million work outside their hometowns, and 94 million work in towns near their home regions.

As peasant workers mostly receive limited education and usually engage in low-skilled jobs, they are representative of low-skilled workers. However, they are different from urban low-skilled workers in some important aspects, namely: (1) peasant workers have farmlands in their rural home regions but the latter do not; under some circumstances (say, living costs in cities are too high to afford), peasant workers can retreat from cities to countryside, but urban low-skilled workers have no choice but live in cities. They may opt for living in slums if they cannot afford to buy or rent apartments in cities; (2) despite these obvious disadvantages, city residents are offered exclusive social securities and welfare, e.g., medical insurance, pension, unemployment insurance, better education opportunities, etc., while peasant workers are excluded from these benefits; (3) peasant workers show periodical mobility, i.e., they usually try hard to ensure annual reunions with their families in the countryside on important seasonal occasions (e.g., Chinese Spring Festival) as they indentify their rural abode as their true home.

As more and more peasant workers migrate into cities, it results in the equalization of nominal wages of peasant workers and urban low-skilled workers. According to the national population sampling survey (1%) in 2005, average wages of peasant workers are very close to that of urban low-skilled workers (Xing 2008). The particularity of China's labor market provides us great convenience in investigating the relationship between city size and nominal wages and living costs of low-skilled workers. Since during the Spring Festival (the most significant annual celebrations in China) most peasant workers return to their home regions from different sized cities to reunite with their families, conducting a survey during the Spring Festival in China's rural villages having large numbers of peasant workers not only saves the time and costs for survey, but also avoids the difficulty of identifying low-skilled workers in cities.

2.3.2 Wages Formation of Peasant Workers

China is a country with a very large agricultural population. It accounts for nearly 40% of the world's agricultural population, but only has 9% of the world's arable lands. The average cultivated land area for Chinese peasant households is only about 7 *mu* (around 0.32 acre), whose limited total productivity for subsistence necessitates the existence of massive surplus labor in China's rural areas. In other words, the marginal agricultural product of adult labor in China's rural areas is as low as close to zero. For this reason, working full-time or part-time in cities will contribute to some net increase in peasants' household income.

China's economy began to revive in 1990s after the country revamped its open-door policies and reform programs in 1992. This was accompanied by a huge demand for labor in the thriving manufacturing sectors in China's coastal cities. Since then, large amounts of surplus labors from China's rural areas (in the form of peasant workers) began to flood into cities. Now, they have accounted for the bulk of increased urban population and become the major forces that drive the urbanization process in China. For instance, in 2010, peasant workers accounted for 35.9% of the total population of Beijing, while the increased population of Beijing consisted mostly of peasant workers. Meanwhile, peasant workers accounted for 77% of the total population of Shenzhen, a megacity adjacent to Hong Kong. Therefore, peasant workers are clearly an important component of Chinese urban labor forces.

According to the labor supply theory of Lewis (1954), firms' decisions on wages are mainly based on the opportunity costs of peasant workers. For peasant workers in cities, their opportunity cost is the marginal contribution of farming at rural home to their household income, which has nothing to do with the size of cities they work in. In principle, firms can hire enough number of peasant workers at a wage just sufficient for their survival in cities. This wage should appropriately compensates for the emotional costs of peasant workers' being far away from home, and cover the costs of physical strength and travel expenses. In practice, however, the nominal wages of peasant workers in China's large cities are so low that they can hardly afford decent dwelling places in these cities.

In spite of poor living conditions that accompany their low income received in large cities, some peasant workers can save enough money to build big "western-style houses" in the countryside after working for many years in cities. Consequently, peasant workers have gradually evolved a life pattern of "earning money in cities, and building houses and consuming in countryside". In the acquaintance society of rural home regions, the psychology of conspicuous consumption among peasant workers on their houses and durable goods has also strengthened this life pattern.

According to the latest statistics (NBS 2012), among 156 million peasant workers who work outside their home regions, those aged above 40 only account for 18.2%. It suggests that peasant workers begin to retreat from the urban labor market when they become 35 years old, and most of them quit after 40 years old. This is not difficult to understand because when they reach 35 years old, they have to get married and resolve other household issues (i.e. build their own houses) in their rural home regions. Although some of them do return to cities for work after building a house and getting married in the countryside, physically they are less competitive compared to younger generation of peasant workers, and their emotional costs also increase greatly. Eventually, only a few peasant workers settle down in cities, and they do not represent the mainstream who follow the life pattern mentioned above. In short, the objectives of peasant workers are confined to "earning money in cities, building houses and consuming in countryside".[5]

Based on the above analysis, the objective function of a typical peasant worker can be denoted as follows:

$$MAX : S = W - C_h - C_n,$$

where S stands for saving (the amount of money they can remit to their home regions), W is nominal wage, C_h is housing costs, and C_n is non-housing living expenses including foods, clothing, services, etc. The nominal wage is determined by market demand and supply, and the peasant worker simply accepts it. In order to maximize his savings, the peasant worker adopts strategies to minimize his total expenses including housing costs and non-housing living expenses (the above equation does not allow for the impact of city amenities, but in the later empirical analysis its impact on workers' wages will be considered).

Peasant workers' objectives of savings maximization lead to basically the similar dwelling pattern of peasant workers in cities. For example, peasant workers in manufacturing industries usually dwell in humble collective dormitories provided by their employers. Housing costs of such dwelling places are low or even gratuitous (e.g. self-employed store owners would dwell in their own stores where they run small business in daytime). Peasant workers engaged in construction work usually dwell in

[5]The younger generation of Chinese peasant workers differ from older generations in their attitude towards living in cities. Many of them would rather live in cities than follow more traditional life pattern.

temporary sheds near construction sites. Many other peasant workers may dwell in shabby apartments in downtown, city suburbs, or even basement of buildings. These places lack necessary public service facilities and hygiene provisions, but offer cheap rents. Since peasant workers have the similar patterns of dwelling consumption, they may face similar housing costs no matter they are in large cities or small cities. Even if housing costs face the peasant workers differ in city size, it should be far smaller than differences in costs of decent housing between large cities and small cities.

The equilibrium condition for peasant workers to flow between large and small cities can be denoted as follows:

$$W^L - W^S = C_h^L - C_h^S \approx 0 \ll C_{dh}^L - C_{dh}^S,$$

where W^L and W^S denote nominal wages of peasant workers in large city L and small city S, respectively. C_h^L and C_h^S denote housing costs of typical peasant workers in large and small cities, and C_{dh}^L and C_{dh}^S denote costs of decent housing in large and small cities. Due to huge differences in house prices between large cities and small cities, C_{dh}^L should be far larger than C_{dh}^S.[6] The authors do not consider non-housing expenses for two reasons. First, most consumer goods (e.g., food, clothing, and daily necessities) are tradable across regions thus have similar prices in different cities. Second, most peasant workers only consume basic services in the cities (e.g., simple haircuts); they rarely spend money on dining in restaurants and entertainment activities such as watching movies. Since the low-end living services do not differ much in price between large and small cities, the aforementioned equation implies that their spending on non-housing consumption can be ignored due to very small differences across cities. This hypothesis will be tested in Sect. 2.4.[7] Specifically, according to the latest statistics (NBS 2012), the average monthly wage of Chinese peasant workers in 2011 was 2,049 yuan. By region, it was 2,053, 2,006, and 1,990 yuan in the eastern, central, and western China regions, respectively. By city type, it was 2,302, 2,041, 2,011, 1,982, and 1,961 in municipalities, provincial capital cities, prefectural cities, county-level cities, and townships, respectively.[8]

The above equilibrium condition has at least two meanings. First, the housing costs for peasant workers should be independent of city size and city housing prices (unlike the huge difference in cost for decent housing between large and small cities

[6]The cost of living for city residents who are eager to live in honorable houses differs greatly between cities of different sizes. For example, in 2009 the cost of housing in Beijing and Shanghai was 13,464 RMB/m^2 and 12,435 RMB/m^2, respectively. Meanwhile, in Suizhou (a medium city in Hubei province), the average housing price was just 1,681 RMB/m^2. According to the authors' own survey, the housing price in Zhongzhou (a small town with population of 5,000 in Hanchuang, Hubei province), is as low as 850 RMB/m^2 in 2012.

[7]The FMR (Fair Market Rents) index released by U.S. Department of Housing and Urban Development which measures the costs of living for the low-income population in different cities also relies on the assumption that non-housing living costs are the same across cities (Curran et al. 2006).

[8]These statistics are based surveys of 200,000 peasant workers from 7,000 villages across China. It is a simple average for all peasant workers, and does not take into account other important information that affects wages such as occupation.

for local, urban residents). Second, the wages of peasant workers should also be independent of city size. Survey data will be used to empirically test these two predictions made from the theoretical analysis below.

2.4 Data and Variables

2.4.1 *About the Survey*

The authors conducted a survey of peasant workers during the 2011 Spring Festival in China. The villages selected for the survey are located in regions where peasant workers account for a high proportion of the total local population. These regions are Jiangyou county (in Sichuan province), Wanjiang county and Lixin county (in Anhui province), Zhijiang county (in Hubei province), Nanchang county (in Jiangxi province), Nan County (in Hunan province), and Puyang county (in Henan province). In addition, the above regions are all located in plains, where peasant workers have similar information and transportation costs as compared to those from mountainous regions.[9]

Stratified random interviews and questionnaires were used for this survey. The interviewers selected two or three townships in each region, and then randomly selected 11–12 villages from each township. In each village, they randomly selected 10–20 farmers for interview. During the interview, interviewers read the questionnaires to the peasant workers or head of the households, then filled in the questionnaires according to their answers. In the end, 1,155 peasant workers were interviewed from 78 villages. After excluding those questionnaires that did not accurately report upon their workplaces, a valid sample of 1,112 peasant workers was obtained.

The information collected by this survey includes nominal wages and various personal characteristics of peasant workers such as their age, gender, education level, occupation, work duration, political status (i.e., CCP member or not), workplaces, etc. All of the cities were divided into three or four categories by size, and thus there are no more than 180 samples for each category. Importantly, most peasant workers are similar in several personal characteristics such as education level (most have only junior middle school or primary school educations), occupations (most are self-employed small business owners, manufacturing workers, and craftsmen). For these two reasons, the sample should be relatively representative for the purposes of this research.

[9]A huge difference in information and transportation costs for peasant workers may exist in mountainous areas due to treacherous transportation conditions.

2.4.2 *Definition of City Size*

Population is often used in literature to define city size, but this method might not be suitable here because of the huge economic inequality across China's regions. Specifically, wage levels and living costs may be quite different across China's cities even if they are of similar size in terms of population. For example, according to the sixth national census of China, the population of Chongqing is 28,846,000, and the population of Shanghai is 23,019,000; yet the housing prices in Chongqing and Shanghai are 3,611 RMB/m^2 and 12,426 RMB/m^2, respectively, due to the different rate of economic development in these two cities. Alternatively, this study employs two other reasonable methods to define city size, but population is used as a measure of city size as a robustness check.

First, city size is defined using house prices. Moulton (1995) pointed out that house price and housing costs are the most important elements causing differences in cost of living across regions. The U.S. Department of Housing and Urban Development's (HUD) Fair Market Rents (FMR) measure also relies on the assumption that housing and utility costs are the only source of cost of living differences among areas or that the other sources of price differences in a region's COL are highly correlated with these costs (Curran et al. 2006). The Chinese Urban Life and Price Year book (2010) reports the average selling prices of houses in prefectural cities in 2009. According to this information, the authors of this article define "megacity", "large city", and "other city" according the following criteria. A "megacity" refers to a city where the average housing price was above 10,000 RMB/m^2; "large city" refers to a city where the average housing price was between 5,000–10,000 RMB/m^2; and "other city" refers to a city where the average housing price was below 5,000 RMB/m^2.[10]

The authors' second measure of city size is based on the administrative level and economic development level of the cities. As economic development in China is largely government-led, cities with higher administrative levels may enjoy preferential economic policies and better development opportunities. They thus have better infrastructures and larger populations and scales. The economic development level of cities is also considered. Peasant workers gather in the cities of southeast China, which are more developed than those in other regions of China. These cities generally have higher costs of living than their counterparts with equivalent administrative levels in other parts of China. According to this criteria, the cities of Beijing, Shanghai, Guangzhou, and Shenzhen, all well-accepted first-tier cities in China, are defined herein as megacities. Chongqing, Suzhou, Foshan, Wenzhou, and vice-provincial level cities excluding Guangzhou and Shenzhen are defined as large cities.

Our second measure of city size is based on the administrative level plus economic development of cities. As economic development in China is largely government-led, which means that cities with higher administrative levels may enjoy preferential economic policies and better development opportunities, thus have better infrastructures and larger population and scale. In addition to administrative level, we also consider the economic development of cities. Because peasant workers heavily gather in cities

[10]See appendix for a complete list of cities with different sizes.

in southeast China, which are more developed than other regions in China. And these cities generally have higher costs of living than their counterparts with equivalent administrative levels in other part of China. According to this criteria, we define Beijing, Shanghai, Guangzhou and Shenzhen, well accepted first-tier cities in China, as *megacity*; define Chongqing, Suzhou, Foshan, Wenzhou, and vice-provincial level cities excluding Guangzhou and Shenzhen as *large city*[11]; define other provincial capital cities in mid-west of China and several big cities famous for their rapid economic development after 1980 in south and east China as *Medium-large cities*[12]; and define the rest cities as *other cities*. See Appendix for a complete list of cities in each size category.[13]

2.4.3 Definition of Occupations

Nominal wages of peasant workers vary substantially with their occupations. Therefore, occupation factor should be allowed in order to investigate the nominal wages of peasant workers. We adopt the vocation classifications of the NBS Census of Agriculture in this study to define 11 occupations of peasant workers: *Self-employed small business owner, professional and technician, managerial staff, general staff, Sales personnel, manufacturing worker, commercial worker, service worker, construction and decoration worker, craftsman*, and *other occupations*. In our sample, the majority of peasant workers are *self-employed small business owners, manufacturing workers and craftsman.*[14]

[11]Although Chongqing is a provincial-level city, the housing price and cost of living there are similar to those of Wuhan, a vice-provincial level city in Hubei province. Suzhou, Wenzhou, and Foshan are prefecture-level cities, but Suzhou (with housing prices higher than Wuhan and a population of more than four million) is close to Shanghai and famous for its rapid post-1980 economic development. Wenzhou, the fastest-growing city in the manufacturing and processing trade, belongs to the category of megacity because its average housing price exceeded 10,000 RMB/m^2 in 2009. Foshan, very near to Guangzhou (and even closer to downtown Guangzhou than the so-called Guangzhou Huadu District) can actually be seen as a sub-center of the Guangzhou metropolitan area. In March of 2009, Guangzhou and Foshan signed the "Agreement of Co-operation between Guangzhou and Foshan", as well as supplemental agreements covering urban planning, transportation infrastructure, and industrial cooperation and environmental protection, which mark the official integration of Guangzhou and Foshan.

[12]Cities in south and east China include Wuxi, Changzhou, Zhenjiang, Yangzhou and Nantong in Jiangsu province, Shaoxing, and Huzhou in Zhejiang province, Dongguan, Zhuhai and Shantou in Guangdong province, Quanzhou and Fuzhou in Fujian province, and Yantai in Shandong province.

[13]Several cities are defined as "other cities" but actually possess relatively high economic development levels when compared to other cities in this category. To allow for the possible misclassification, "medium-large cities" and "other cities" are redefined in Sect. 2.4 as a robustness.

[14]See Appendix for a detailed description of these 11 occupations.

2.4.4 Variables Description

(1) Workplaces of peasant workers

Of the 1,155 surveyed peasant workers, 338 workers work in their home province while 809 workers work in other provinces. It shows that more than 70% of peasant workers work in other provinces, among which there are 629 people working in eastern cities. Table 2.1 shows a sample distribution of peasant workers in the different types of cities as defined above. According to Table 2.1, about 20% of peasant workers reside in megacities, 20% in large cities, and the rest live in smaller cities.

(2) Wages of peasant workers

1,079 peasant workers reported their monthly average wages in this survey. The average total is 2,639 yuan with a standard deviation of 1,836, including 25 peasant workers whose monthly nominal wages have reached 8,000 RMB. These peasant workers are considered to be outliers. Table 2.2 presents a summary of monthly wage and housing cost statistics affecting peasant workers in different types of cities. The average monthly wage of peasant workers varies from 2,200 to 2,600 RMB in different types of cities, while housing costs range between 181 and 305 RMB.

(3) Personal characteristics of the peasant workers

Two of the 1,079 peasant workers surveyed herein admitted to being illiterate. 195 (or 16.9%) reported completing a primary school education, with 790 (68.3%) finishing junior high school and 72 graduating high school. Another 45 reported finishing a technical secondary school education, with 25 finishing junior college and 29 others earning some degree of higher education. This indicates that illiterate peasant workers are almost non-existent, and the majority of peasant workers have primary and junior middle school education.

Among the surveyed peasant workers are 231 *self-employed small business owners*, 35 *professionals and technicians*, 15 *managerial staffs*, 51 *general staffs*, 25

Table 2.1 Sample size of surveyed peasant workers who work in different types of cities

City definition 1 (by housing prices)	Megacities	Large cities	Other cities	
	273	216	623	
City definition 2 (by administrative levels)	Megacities	Large cities	Medium-large cities	Other cities
	203	183	271	455

Note According to city definition 1, Megacity, large city, and other city differ in their housing price levels, and are defined as cities whose overall housing prices in 2009 above 10,000 RMB, between 5000 and 10000 RMB, below 5000 RMB, respectively; According to city definition 2, Megacity, large city, big city, and other city differ in their administrative levels, and basically correspond to municipality, provincial capital city, prefectural city, and county-level city, respectively

Table 2.2 Descriptive statistics of wages and dwelling costs of peasant workers in China (based on survey sample)

		Wage			Dwelling cost		
		Mean	Median	St. dev.	Mean	Median	St. dev.
City definition 1 (by housing price)	Megacity	2626	2000	1393	289	120	354
	Large city	2527	2500	1072	279	100	336
	Other city	2411	2000	1148	260	100	315
City definition 2 (by administrative level)	Megacity	2626	2000	1393	305	120	378
	Large city	2551	2500	1019	282	150	323
	Medium-large city	2196	2000	1149	181	0	268
	Other city	2446	2200	1165	273	100	326

Table 2.3 Ages and work duration of surveyed peasant workers

	Mean	Median	Max	Min value	St. dev.
Age	30.9	29	68	15	9.5
Work duration	4.1	3	30	0.3	3.7

sales personnels, 215 *manufacturing workers*, 36 *commercial workers*, 57 *service workers*, 110 *construction and decoration workers*, 212 *craftsman*, and 152 who engage in *other occupations*. Additionally, 753 are male, and 26 are Chinese Communist Party (hereinafter "CCP") members. Table 2.3 presents the age and work tenure statistics of the peasant workers

2.5 Empirical Analysis

2.5.1 Impacts of City Size on Nominal Wages

The following econometric model is employed to estimate the effects of city size on the nominal wages of peasant workers in different cities:

$$\begin{aligned}\ln wage =& \beta_0 + \theta * AMSIZE + \beta_1 prov + \beta_2 county + \beta_3 age + \beta_4 age2 \\ & + \beta_5 time + \beta_6 time2 + \beta_7 gend + \beta_8 party + \beta_9 health \\ & + \beta_{10} married + \beta_{11} together + \lambda * EDU + \gamma * OCC + \varepsilon,\end{aligned} \tag{2.15}$$

"*wage*" refers to monthly wage of peasant workers. Both monthly wages and hourly wages have been used to measure wage levels in the existing literature, but in our sample the peasant workers reported their monthly wages. It is difficult to calculate hourly wages because peasant workers are often required to work overtime.

"*AMSIZE*" is a group of dummy variables indicating the types of city size. In the first measure, city size is classified into three types: *amsizeA*1 (megacity), *amsizeA*2 (large city), and *amsizeA*3 (other city). In the second measure, city size is subdivided into four types: *amsizeB*1 (megacity), *amsizeB*2 (large city), *amsizeB*3 (medium-large city), and *amsizeB*4 (other city). Note that using city dummies have an important advantage, i.e., it not only captures the city scale but also reflects city amenities. It is of our key interest to examine whether the estimates of *AMSIZE* significantly differ from 0 or not. In other words, we test whether the nominal wages of peasant workers are significantly different in different sized cities with different amenity degrees.

"*prov*" is a dummy variable indicating whether a peasant works outside of his home province, and "*county*" is a dummy variable indicating whether a peasant works in his home province but outside of his home county. Specifically, *prov* equals 1 if he works outside his home province, and *prov* equals 0 otherwise; *county* equals 1 if he works in his home province but outside his home county, and county equals 0 otherwise. These two variables are controlled in the model for two reasons. First, distance of work place should affect the wages of peasant workers wage. For example, working in a city far away from hometown means higher transportation costs and emotional burdens due to fewer chances to reunite with their families. Second, capability of a peasant worker may affect both his wages and location choice. Omitting such a variable in the regression will cuase endogenous problem and lead to estimation bias. Since capability is unobservable, we proxy for it using these two variables. This method is based on the assumption that survival in an more alien land (in term of distance to hometown) needs more skills and capability.

The variables *age* and *age*2 refer to age and square of age, respectively. Adding "age-squared" into regression assumes an inverted "U" shape relationship between the age and wage of peasant workers. This should be intuitive because most peasant workers take part in jobs that rely on physical strength, and physical strength declines with age. Meanwhile, although workers may be more energetic in their youth, they also lack experience and that limits their earning potential. The variables *time* and *time*2 refer to the number of years worked in their reported vocations; time, to some extent, reflects the skill of peasant workers. The authors of this paper have chosen to follow the literature and insert "time-squared" into the regression (Combes et al. 2012). The term gend is a dummy variable indicating the gender of peasant workers ($gend = 1$ if male, otherwise $gend = 0$). The term party is dummy variable indicating whether the peasant worker is a CCP member. Generally, only capable persons can join the CCP in the countryside, and thus CCP membership should to some extent reflect the ability of peasant workers. The term *EDU* represents a group of dummy variables indicating the maximum education level of the peasant workers, i.e., whether they attended junior middle school, high school, technical secondary school, junior college, or college. Meanwhile, *VOC* is a group of dummy variables indicating whether peasant workers engage in certain occupations. The terms *health*, *married*, and *together* are dummy variables indicating health status (1 if good health, 0 if otherwise), marital status (1 if married, 0 if otherwise), and whether or not they are together with their spouse (1 if yes, 0 if otherwise).

Table 2.4 reports the OLS estimation results of Model 1. Columns 1–3 show the results when the first method of city size definition is employed, and Columns 4–5 demonstrate the results when the second method of city size definition is used. Column 1 reveals that city size dummies are insignificant, which implies that there are no significant wage differences for peasant workers across cities where housing prices are different (i.e., the first measure of city size). Column 2–3 shows that the wages of peasant workers may be affected as more factors are controlled for, but that city size dummies remain insignificant, which further reinforces the finding in Column 1. The city size definition is changed in Columns 4–6, revealing that city size dummies are insignificant (and may even be significantly negative in Column 4), implying that the nominal wages of peasant workers in megacities, large cities, and medium-large cities are no higher (if not lower) than those in other cities in terms of the second measure of city size. For *prov* and *county*, the estimated coefficients are positive and mostly significant in all columns, indicating that peasant workers who work outside their native counties and provinces usually obtain higher wages than those who remain in their hometowns. This is because of compensation for both higher emotional and transportation costs, as well as the fact that the workers likely possess higher ability levels that place them in wider demand. The coefficients of *age* and *age*2 are highly in-line with the predicted result, i.e., that wages initially increase with age but decrease over time, governed by an inverted U-shape relationship between the ages and wages of peasant workers. In addition, male peasant workers earn higher wages than females as shown in positive coefficients of *gend*. Wages also increase with the length of engaging in an occupation as shown in the positive coefficient of *time* (note that *time*2 is insignificant in all cases). Having CCP membership also significantly increases the wages of peasant workers. Health status and marriage status have no apparent impact on the wages of peasant workers, and being together with a spouse actually significantly decreases a peasant worker's wages, perhaps due to the lower emotional cost of employment.

It is of concern that capable peasant workers often choose to work in large cities, resulting in a high correlation between city size and human resource ability levels (partially proxied by *prov* and *county*). The empirical strategy used herein to eliminate such an impact is running a regression for only a sub-sample of peasant workers who work outside of their home provinces. The regression results are shown in Table 2.5. The results therein are consistent with those found in Table 2.4, i.e., that city size dummies are insignificant in both city size measures and after controlling for additional variables in the regressions.

Table 2.4 Regression results of Model 1

(Explained variable: the logarithm of the *wage*)

	1	2	3	4	5	6
Age		0.028*** (2.69)	0.030*** (3.78)		0.030*** (2.86)	0.032*** (2.68)
age2		−0.000*** (3.07)	−0.000*** (2.92)		−0.000*** (3.27)	−0.001*** (3.16)
Gend		0.094*** (3.77)	0.084*** (3.31)		0.092*** (3.55)	0.082*** (3.10)
Party		0.158* (1.81)	0.155* (1.78)		0.158** (1.79)	0.153* (1.75)
SizeA1	−0.050 (1.26)	0.047 (1.32)	0.051 (1.43)			
SizeA2	−0.013 (0.33)	0.037 (1.13)	0.026 (0.77)			
SizeB1				−0.055 (0.16)	0.023 (0.55)	0.031 (0.72)
SizeB2				−0.078 (0.78)	0.033 (0.89)	0.036 (0.96)
SizeB3				−0.069* (1.69)	−0.007 (0.20)	−0.015 (0.41)
Time		0.030*** (3.31)	0.033*** (3.47)		0.031*** (3.27)	0.033*** (3.42)
Time2		−0.000 (1.03)	0.001 (1.18)		−0.000 (1.02)	−0.001 (1.15)
Prov	0.262*** (5.87)	0.216*** (5.56)	0.220** (5.63)	0.276*** (5.88)	0.235*** (5.68)	0.236*** (5.66)
County	0.075 (1.57)	0.121*** (2.92)	0.123*** (2.98)	0.119** (2.10)	0.126*** (2.65)	0.134*** (2.81)
Health			0.011 (0.048)			0.002 (0.009)
Married			0.055 (1.18)			0.041 (0.86)
Together			−0.082** (2.03)			−0.073* (1.77)
Edu. dummies	No	Yes	Yes	No	Yes	Yes
Occup. dummies	No	Yes	Yes	No	Yes	Yes
Adj. R2	0.046	0.382	0.374	0.045	0.376	0.367
N of obs.	990	943	929	959	915	901

Note t-statistics are in parenthesis; ***, **, and * denote significance level of 1%, 5%, and 10%, respectively

Results are similar if age2 are excluded from the regressions 2–3, 5–6

Table 2.5 Sub-sample regression results of Model 1 (peasant workers outside home province) (Explained variable: the logarithm of the *wage*)

	7	8	9	10	11	12
Age		0.030** (2.39)	0.033** (2.42)		0.032*** (2.64)	0.037*** (2.72)
age2		−0.001*** (2.85)	−0.001*** (2.76)		−0.001*** (3.18)	−0.001*** (3.14)
Gend		0.042 (1.47)	0.028 (0.99)		0.041 (1.38)	0.029 (0.96)
Party		0.041 (0.37)	0.131 (0.27)		0.042 (0.36)	0.032 (0.27)
SizeA1	−0.059 (1.52)	0.028 (0.77)	0.025 (0.70)			
SizeA2	−0.021 (0.50)	0.021 (0.59)	0.028 (0.99)			
SizeB1				−0.017 (0.36)	0.012 (0.26)	0.010 (0.23)
SizeB2				0.001 (0.01)	0.045 (1.17)	0.043 (1.10)
SizeB3				0.013 (0.25)	0.005 (0.12)	−0.006 (0.12)
Time		0.032*** (2.72)	0.032*** (2.58)		0.032*** (2.69)	0.031** (2.53)
Time2		−0.001 (1.32)	−0.001 (1.19)		0.001 (1.32)	−0.001 (1.16)
Health			0.116 (0.49)			0.086 (0.37)
Married			−0.005 (0.09)			−0.021 (0.36)
Together			−0.044 (0.82)			−0.029 (0.52)
Edu. dummies	No	Yes	Yes	No	Yes	Yes
Occup. dummies	No	Yes	Yes	No	Yes	Yes
Adj. R2	0.001	0.356	0.341	−0.004	0.348	0.332
N of obs.	665	631	617	635	604	590

Note t-statistics are in parenthesis; ***, **, and * denote significance level of 1%, 5%, and 10%, respectively
Results are similar if age2 are excluded from the regressions 2–3, 5–6

2.5.2 *Impacts of City Size on Housing Costs*

The theoretical analysis in Sect. 2.2 posited that because the bargaining power of low-skill workers is relatively weak in wage negotiation, they are unable to realize a sufficient wage to cover the cost of respectable living housing in urban areas. They often must accept low-wage jobs and reside in slums in order to make a living. The housing costs and living costs of low-skill workers may therefore be similar across different cities. In other words, city size makes little difference in the nominal wages of low-skill workers.

An idiosyncrasy of China's labor market is that even though low-skill peasant workers hardly receive a wage that covers the cost of decent city life, their pay is sufficient to buy decent housing in the countryside. As a result, many peasant workers gradually following living pattern of "earning money in cities and building houses in the countryside". Their aim is to work in a city and save as much money as possible so that they can return to a respectable house and lifestyle in their hometown. Therefore, we can infer that the housing costs and living costs do not differ much for peasant workers no matter the scale of the city in which they work in. This inference has been empirically tested. The following econometric model was used to estimate the effects of city size on housing costs for peasant workers in different sized cities:

$$hc = \beta_0 + \theta * AMSIZE + \beta * X + \gamma wage + \varepsilon \tag{2.16}$$

Variable *hc* represents the housing costs for peasant workers. As mentioned above, the housing costs of many migrant workers is zero, and so the real value of housing costs is used herein instead of a logarithm. Variable *X* is a vector of characteristics variables that may affect the housing costs of peasant workers, including age, gender, political affiliation (i.e., CCP member or not), education level, occupation, workplace (i.e., province, county), health, marriage status, and whether or not they are cohabitating with their spouse. Wage is also an important determinant of housing costs, and is thus included in the regression model.

Table 2.6 displays the regression results of Model 2. Columns 1–3 show the regression results using the first measure of city size, while Columns 4–6 report the results using the second measure of city size. Control variables are added step-by-step into the first and second regressions, and then focus on a sub-sample of peasant workers who work outside of their home provinces in the third regression. Columns 2–3 seem to indicate that, in terms of the first measure, peasant workers living in large cities pay an average additional housing cost of 48–72 RMB per month than those living in smaller cities. As the median monthly wage of a peasant worker is roughly 2,000 RMB, this additional amount is fairly trivial (accounting for only 2.4–3.6% of income). Columns 4–6 demonstrate that city size estimate dummies are insignificant in all three regressions, indicating that peasant worker housing costs do not differ much across cities, at least in terms of the second city size measure. Actually, all of the megacity dummies are insignificant in Columns 1–6, implying that the housing costs of peasant workers in megacities is no higher than that of small cities. Based on this evidence, it may be generally concluded that city size does not pose a significant difference in housing costs for peasant workers. However, the results show that the wage received significantly contributes to the housing costs of peasant workers, which is also in-line with expectations.

Table 2.6 Regression results of model 2: dwelling costs

	1	2	3	4	5	6
Age		−1.359 (1.13)	−0.031 (0.02)		−1.090 (0.87)	0.253 (0.15)
Gend		−32.47* (1.74)	−23.63 (1.08)		−38.84** (2.05)	−27.73 (1.23)
Party		67.94 (0.79)	−53.11 (0.57)		74.86 (0.86)	−46.46 (0.48)
SizeA1	−15.38 (0.45)	17.10 (0.65)	−4.455 (0.17)			
SizeA2	27.24 (0.77)	73.98*** (2.87)	47.77* (1.83)			
SizeB1				−23.25 (0.60)	2.431 (0.08)	−4.107 (0.13)
SizeB2				−25.95 (0.65)	24.53 (0.86)	28.66 (1.01)
SizeB3				−8.880 (0.26)	10.18 (0.38)	26.97 (0.85)
Prov	227.8*** (5.97)	87.32*** (3.42)		245.2*** (6.09)	109.2*** (3.90)	
County	147.7*** (3.63)	40.96* (1.53)		154.2** (3.34)	35.31 (1.06)	
Wage		0.106*** (7.74)	0.106*** (6.53)		0.103*** (7.52)	0.103*** (6.23)
Health		185.6*** (3.97)	173.6** (2.56)		197.8*** (4.08)	180.6** (2.50)
Married		−29.65 (0.87)	−83.17** (2.10)		−42.85 (1.21)	−99.98** (2.43)
Together		77.65*** (2.66)	126.6*** (3.69)		84.42*** (2.82)	136.9*** (3.85)
Edu. dummies	No	Yes	Yes	No	Yes	Yes
Occup. dummies	No	Yes	Yes	No	Yes	Yes
Adj. R2	0.045	0.404	0.392	0.043	0.392	0.381
N of obs.	995	943	623	964	912	593

Note t-statistics are in parenthesis; *** , **, and * denote significance level of 1%, 5%, and 10%, respectively. Results are similar if age2 are included in the regressions. The results are similar when variables health, married, and together are excluded from the regressions

Table 2.7 Regression results of model 3: living costs other than housing

	1	2	3	4	5	6
Age		−0.995 (0.59)	−0.723 (0.35)		−2.484 (1.46)	−1.070 (0.51)
Gend		24.99 (0.90)	21.20 (0.71)		20.82 (0.73)	16.69 (0.54)
Party		134.5 (1.46)	124.6 (0.73)		114.2 (1.01)	110.5 (0.71)
SizeA1	116.8** (2.43)	39.39 (0.97)	42.33 (1.02)			
SizeA2	−46.29 (0.91)	−47.73 (1.43)	−51.52 (1.45)			
SizeB1				105.1* (1.92)	41.14 (0.96)	49.35 (1.13)
SizeB2				40.38 (0.72)	73.24* (1.87)	68.14* (1.70)
SizeB3				−41.98 (0.85)	−17.48 (0.52)	−2.986 (0.07)
Prov	66.17 (1.23)	−39.64 (0.82)		56.97 (1.01)	−78.17* (1.67)	
County	−5.890 (0.11)	−73.46 (1.49)		19.26 (0.30)	−77.82 (1.47)	
wage		0.192*** (9.73)	0.177*** (8.41)		0.192*** (9.65)	0.175*** (8.30)
Health		−263.9 (1.37)	−59.67 (0.33)		−297.4* (1.66)	−129.3 (0.78)
Married		−116.6** (2.55)	−136.8** (2.56)		−99.82** (2.21)	−129.5** (2.55)
Together		37.79 (0.91)	16.99 (0.37)		54.92 (1.32)	57.31 (1.29)
Edu. dummies	No	Yes	Yes	No	Yes	Yes
Occup. dummies	No	Yes	Yes	No	Yes	Yes
Adj. R2	0.018	0.267	0.269	0.012	0.269	0.270
N of obs.	904	870	563	875	841	535

Note OTE: t-statistics are in parenthesis; ***, **, and * denote significance level of 1%, 5%, and 10%, respectively. Results are similar if age2 are included in the regressions. The results are similar when variables health, married, and together are excluded from the regressions

2.5.3 *Impacts of City Size on Non-housing Living Costs*

It is also of interest to estimate the effect of city size on the non-housing living costs for peasant workers, which accounts for a large portion of their living expenses.[15] The econometric model we employ is as follows.

$$olc = \beta_0 + \theta * AMSIZE + \beta * X + \gamma wage + \varepsilon, \tag{2.17}$$

Variable *olc* represents the non-housing living costs, while other variables are the equivalents of those used in Model 2. As Columns 1–3 of Table 2.7 show, estimates of city size dummies are mostly insignificant where the first city size measure is used (despite the positive and significant estimate of megacity (*amsizeA*1) in Column 1). If the additional controls for living expense are included in the regressions (i.e., the full sample used in Column 2, and the subsample of peasant workers in non-home provinces used in Column 3), both city dummies (*amsizeA*1 and *amsizeA*2) become insignificant. This means that the non-housing costs of living for peasant workers barely differ from city to city. Column 4 demonstrates that megacities have higher non-housing living costs than the benchmark cities (namely *other cities*) in terms of the second measure of city size. As Columns 5–6 show, when more controls are put into the regressions, the non-housing living costs in large cities are a bit higher on average (i.e., 86–88 RMB) than that in other cities, but the magnitude of coefficients is trivial (accounting for only 4.3–4.4% of the median monthly wages of peasant workers). Based on the above regression analysis, it can be concluded that the cost of living is basically the same for peasant workers residing in megacities, large cities, medium-large cities, and other cities.

2.6 Robustness Checks

(1) Controlling for zero housing costs and zero non-housing costs

In our sample, 452 peasant workers reported no housing cost, which means that they either live at the worksite or nearby dormitories provided by their employers. Although free lodging reduces their financial burden to some extent, it is likely that they receive this benefit at the price of receiving a lower wage due to their weak bargaining power in the labor market. This concern is addressed by further controlling for the possible impact of free housing in the baseline regression, and thus the new regression model is as follows:

$$\ln wage = \beta_0 + \theta * AMSIZE + \beta * X + \gamma dhc + \varepsilon, \tag{2.18}$$

[15] A 10% decrease in sample size is suffered here as some peasant workers either did not report or incorrectly reported their non-housing living expenses.

Table 2.8 Robustness check 1: controlling for free housing and zero living costs

(Explained variable: the logarithm of the *wage*)

	1	2	3	4	5	6
Age	0.033*** (3.14)	0.031*** (2.95)	0.034*** (2.82)	0.038*** (3.48)	0.035*** (3.24)	0.040*** (3.17)
age2	−0.001*** (3.47)	−0.000*** (3.23)	−0.001*** (3.18)	−0.001*** (3.75)	−0.001*** (3.45)	−0.001*** (3.45)
Gend	0.090*** (3.58)	0.092*** (3.78)	0.036 (1.33)	0.086*** (3.29)	0.088*** (3.49)	0.024 (0.87)
Party	0.157** (1.80)	0.159** (1.83)	0.049 (0.45)	0.209** (2.36)	0.207** (2.31)	0.127 (1.03)
SizeA1		0.066* (1.87)	0.049 (1.37)		0.052 (1.43)	0.038 (1.09)
SizeA2		0.046 (1.42)	0.030 (0.91)		0.014 (0.42)	0.000 (0.00)
SizeB1	0.033 (0.76)			0.012 (0.27)		
SizeB2	0.040 (1.12)			−0.006 (0.16)		
SizeB3	0.001 (0.04)			−0.037 (1.01)		
Time	0.026*** (2.80)	0.025*** (2.83)	0.025** (2.18)	0.027** (2.76)	0.027*** (2.81)	0.030*** (2.71)
Time2	−0.000 (0.69)	−0.000 (0.69)	−0.001 (0.98)	−0.000 (0.84)	−0.000 (0.86)	−0.001 (1.62)
Prov	0.227*** (5.25)	0.202*** (5.03)		0.265*** (6.03)	0.233** (5.61)	
County	0.118** (2.48)	0.117*** (2.82)		0.159** (3.26)	0.138*** (3.24)	
dhc	−0.036 (1.30)	−0.040 (1.47)	−0.041 (1.24)			
dlc				−0.101** (2.06)	0.103** (2.16)	−0.078 (1.00)
Edu. dummies	Yes	Yes	Yes	yes	Yes	Yes
Occup. dummies	Yes	Yes	Yes	yes	Yes	Yes
Adj. R2	0.392	0.399	0.378	0.407	0.415	0.399
N of obs.	895	923	611	831	857	557

Term *dhc* is a dummy variable indicating whether a peasant worker's reported housing cost is zero or not. Other variables in the regression are the same as those used in Model 1. The regression results are reported in Columns 1–3 of Table 2.8. As those Columns show, when the zero housing cost dummy (*dhc*) is introduced to the regressions, the coefficient estimates of *AMSIZE* are still insignificant for both city size measures, which is consistent with the baseline estimation results of Model 1.

The conclusion that city sizes does not affect the nominal wages of peasant workers after controlling for housing costs is based on three reasons. First, the estimates of city size dummies derived from a sub-sample of peasant workers working outside of their home provinces (as shown in Column 3 of Table 2.8) are more convincing because the abilities of and emotional costs upon the peasant workers have also been controlled for. According to the NBS statistics (2012), the majority of peasant workers from central and western China flow into other provinces for work (the 66% figure in this research is highly consistent with the NBS-reported proportions of 67.2% and 57% for the central and western provinces, respectively). Second, the estimates of city size dummies using the second measure of city size are all insignificant, as shown in Column 1 of Table 2.8. Third, although the megacity dummy is significant in Column 2, the magnitude of wage differences reflected between megacities and the benchmark is trivial when compared to the medium wage of peasant workers (6.6% * 2000 = 132), and is far less than the housing price in megacities.

Some peasant workers in our sample are provided with free accommodations aside from free lodging, which may also impact their nominal wage received. To address this concern, the possible impact of free accommodations is controlled in the baseline regression by using the following model:

$$\ln wage = \beta_0 + \theta * AMSIZE + \beta * X + \gamma lhc + \varepsilon, \tag{2.19}$$

Term *lhc* is a dummy variable indicating whether the cost of living reported by a peasant worker is zero or not. The estimation results are reported in Columns 4–6 of Table 2.8. They show that free accommodation significantly reduces the nominal wages of peasant workers, which is in line with our expectation. Despite this fact, however, the city size dummies estimates are insignificant in all three columns, indicating that city size still does not impact the nominal wages of peasant workers even after the free accommodation factor is controlled for.

(2) Using alternative definitions of city size

The two alternative definitions of city size are applied as another robustness check. The method used by Baum-Snow and Pavan (2011) is followed first, i.e., where city size is defined solely by population. According to the sixth Chinese national population census, a megacity (*amsizeC*1) is defined as a city having a population over 10 million; a large city (*amsizeC*2) as having a population between 3 and 10 million; a medium-large city (*amsizeC*3) as having a population between 1 and 3 million; and "other city" (*amsizeC*4) as having a population below 1 million. A complete list of cities is available in the appendix.

A typical prefectural city in China consists of city-administrated districts (qu) and city-administrated counties (xian). City-administrated counties are mostly comprised of rural areas rather than urban ones, thus would be inappropriate to take their rural population into account when calculating city population and scale. Therefore, the

Table 2.9 Robustness check 2: third measure of city size

(Explained variable: the logarithm of the *wage*)						
	1	2	3	4	5	6
Age	0.031*** (2.98)	0.034*** (3.28)	0.040*** (3.66)	0.033*** (2.67)	0.038*** (3.14)	0.045*** (3.61)
age2	−0.001*** (3.39)	−0.001*** (3.62)	−0.001*** (3.90)	−0.001*** (3.18)	−0.001*** (3.56)	−0.001*** (3.94)
Gend	0.091*** (3.50)	0.088*** (3.49)	0.087*** (3.30)	0.041 (1.38)	0.035 (1.22)	0.023 (0.79)
Party	0.154* (1.76)	0.153* (1.76)	0.202** (2.78)	0.046 (0.39)	0.051 (0.45)	0.134 (1.06)
SizeC1	0.010 (0.22)	0.016 (0.36)	0.003 (0.06)	0.011 (0.24)	0.019 (0.40)	0.006 (0.12)
SizeC2	0.011 (0.31)	0.019 (0.54)	−0.014 (0.40)	0.019 (0.46)	0.024 (0.61)	0.016 (0.38)
SizeC3	−0.038 (1.02)	−0.044 (1.17)	−0.064 (1.63)	0.025 (0.53)	0.015 (0.32)	0.003 (0.07)
Time	0.029*** (3.16)	0.153* (1.76)	0.025*** (2.61)	0.032*** (2.66)	0.025** (2.12)	0.031*** (2.66)
Time2	−0.000 (0.93)	−0.000 (0.60)	−0.000 (0.71)	−0.001 (1.30)	−0.001 (0.99)	−0.001 (1.63)
Prov	0.241*** (5.80)	0.236*** (5.36)	0.271*** (6.29)			
County	0.136** (2.90)	0.135*** (2.86)	0.170*** (3.53)			
dhc		−0.035 (1.26)			−0.037 (1.04)	–
dlc			−0.105** (2.17)			−0.069 (0.85)
Edu. dummies	yes	yes	Yes	Yes	Yes	Yes
Occup. dummies	yes	yes	Yes	Yes	Yes	Yes
Adj. R2	0.376	0.393	0.409	0.345	0.365	0.386
N of obs.	911	891	827	601	581	529

Note t-statistics are in parenthesis; ***, **, and * denote significance level of 1%, 5%, and 10%, respectively. The results are similar when variables health, married, and together are included in the regressions

population of urban cities counted by China's statistical department only includes the population of city-administrated districts. This measure is adopted herein. In addition, there are many county-level cities in China. For the purposes of this research, only the population of the city-centers is calculated.

Table 2.9 shows the wage regression results upon using the third definition of city size. Columns 1–6 demonstrate that the three city-size dummies remain insignificant regardless of whether the regression sample is confined to peasant workers working outside of their home province, or whether free housing and living costs are controlled in the regression. This means that the findings are robust to this alternative measure of city size.

Second, the fourth measure of city size was used as a robustness check. This measure is based on the second measure but differs in the definition of "*medium-large*" and "*other*" cities. Specifically, Zhongshan and Huizhou in Guangdong province, Jiaxing in Zhejiang province, and Weihai in Shangdong province (which are large in

Table 2.10 Robustness check 3: fourth measure of city size

(Explained variable: the logarithm of the *wage*)

	1	2	3	4	5	6
Age	0.030*** (2.83)	0.033*** (3.12)	0.038*** (3.47)	0.032*** (2.63)	0.037*** (3.13)	0.044*** (3.59)
age2	−0.001*** (3.25)	−0.001*** (3.45)	−0.001*** (3.72)	−0.001*** (3.16)	−0.001*** (3.58)	−0.001*** (3.93)
Gend	0.092*** (3.57)	0.090*** (3.59)	0.087*** (3.32)	0.041 (1.38)	0.035 (1.23)	0.023 (0.80)
Party	0.158* (1.80)	0.158* (1.81)	0.209** (2.35)	0.043 (0.38)	0.048 (0.43)	0.132 (1.03)
SizeD1	0.033 (0.75)	0.042 (0.94)	0.017 (0.37)	0.022 (0.48)	0.034 (0.72)	0.008 (0.17)
SizeD2	0.045 (1.19)	0.052 (1.40)	0.003 (0.08)	0.057 (1.42)	0.063 (1.60)	0.008 (0.20)
SizeD3	0.006 (0.16)	0.013 (0.36)	−0.028 (0.75)	0.020 (0.45)	0.029 (0.68)	−0.018 (0.41)
Time	0.031*** (3.28)	0.026*** (2.81)	0.027*** (2.76)	0.032*** (2.65)	0.025** (2.11)	0.032*** (2.70)
Time2	−0.000 (1.01)	−0.000 (0.68)	−0.000 (0.85)	−0.001 (1.25)	−0.001 (0.93)	−0.001* (1.67)
Prov	0.230*** (5.38)	0.221*** (4.97)	0.265*** (5.83)			
County	0.120** (2.51)	0.112** (2.35)	0.156*** (3.18			
dhc		−0.036 (1.29)			−0.035 (0.97)	–
dlc			−0.102** (2.08)			−0.071 (0.87)
Edu. dummies	yes	Yes	Yes	Yes	Yes	Yes
Occup. dummies	yes	Yes	Yes	Yes	Yes	Yes
Adj. R2	0.376	0.392	0.407	0.348	0.368	0.388
N of obs.	915	895	831	604	584	532

Note t-statistics are in parenthesis; ***, **, and * denote significance level of 1%, 5%, and 10%, respectively

The results are similar when variables health, married, and together are included in the regressions scale and feature relatively high economic development, yet defined as other cities in the second measure), are classified as "*medium-large* " cities in this measure while keeping all other cities unchanged.

Table 2.10 shows the wage regression results using the fourth measure of city size. The results in Columns 1–6 are consistent with the previous finding that the nominal wages of peasant workers are the same across cities, and they are robust as regards the fourth measure of city size.

2.7 Conclusions and Policy Implication

Through quantitative analysis of survey data collected from peasant workers in China, and this study reveals that the nominal wages and living costs of Chinese peasant workers are essentially identical across cities of different sizes. This finding suggests that the bargaining power of low-skilled Chinese workers is too weak to transfer the high living costs in large cities to their employers by demanding a reasonably high nominal wage. As a result, the agglomeration economies and agglomeration diseconomies are misallocated between firms and workers, and the market mechanisms that normally limit the size of cities (such as rising housing prices and non-housing living expenses) fail to work. In the past decades, firms located in Chinese large cities enjoy more benefits from agglomeration economies but bear less costs from agglomeration diseconomies. The continuous investment in large cities creates large amounts of jobs and leads to the large influx of rural laborers who are in serious need for jobs and willing to accept a subsistence wage. This phenomenon is a crucial impetus for the over-expansion of megacities in the case of China.

Moreover, current government policies also play an important role in fueling this phenomenon. Chinese central and local governments usually invest heavily in infrastructures of large cities and megacities, which is conducive to increasing the attractiveness of these cities to both firms and laborers. However, such policies fail to solve the income and livelihood issues of low-skilled workers in large cities, which helps to perpetuate their difficulties in affording better urban lifestyles.

The most important implication of this study is that market mechanism that maintain the efficient size of a city as well as allocate capital and population effectively across geographical regions may not work in some circumstance, therefore, government intervention is needed in order to prevent over-expansion of megacities in China. Some effective measures should be taken by governments to solve this problem, e.g., offering more training to low-skilled migrant workers in large cities to improve their human capital and wages; and more investments and incentives should be directed to medium and small-sized cities to improve their amenities, so that they become more attractive to firms and laborers.

Admittedly, there are some limitations of this study. First, our research is based on a survey data collected in 2011, but things changed a lot in recent years, which means our conclusions may not be appied to current situation of China. In the past several years, wages and labor costs of migrant workers rose dramatically and many firms are leaving megacities, especially cities in southeastern areas. Second, with the very rapid expansion of large cities in recent years, land prices in these cities also were rising quickly, further squeezing the profits of manufacturing firms which absorb a large proportion of migrant workers in cities, while real estate related firms are prosperous instead. Third, the role of institution is not allowed for in this study, for example, even if a migrant worker could offford the high housing prices in cities, Hukou system restricted them from buying any property and settle down in first-tier and some second-tier large cities.

Appendix A: List of Cities with Different Size Measures

1. City list according to the first measure of city sizes

Megacities (house price above10,000 RMB/SM): Beijing, Shanghai, Guangzhou, Shenzhen, Hangzhou (in *Zhejiang*), Wenzhou (in *Zhejiang*).

Large cities (house price in 5,000–10,000 RMB/SM): Xiamen, Quanzhou (in *Fujian*), Zhuhai, Dongguan, Fushan (in *Guangdong*), Wuhan (in *Hubei*), Nanjing, Wuxi, Suzhou, Yangzhou (in *Jiangsu*), Dalian(in *Liaonin*), Jinan, Qingdao (in *Shandong*), Tianjin, Chengdu (in *Sichuan*), Ningbo, Jiaxing, Huzhou, Shaoxing (in *Zhejiang*).

Other cities: ***Anhui province***: Huaibei, MaAnshan, Chaohu, Fuyang, Bengbu, Hefei, Taihe, Anqing, Wangjiang, Huainan, Wuhu, Dangshan, Huaining. ***Chongqin*** *City*. ***Fujiang***: Zhangzhou, Jinjiang. ***Gansu***: Tianshui. ***Guangdong***: Zhongshan, Shantou, Huizhou, Shipai, Zhanjiang, Maoming. ***Guangxi***: Nanning, Yulin. ***Hebei***: Shenzhou, Shijiazhuang. ***Heilongjian***: Jiamusi. ***Hena***: Hebi, Anyang, Zhoukou, Zhenzhou, Kaifeng, Puyang city, Puyang County, Pingdingshan, Luoyang, Changhuan. ***Hubei***: Xianning, Yichang, Shashi, Yidu, Jingzhou, Zhijiang, Xishui, ***Hunan***: Chenzhou, Nanxian, Changsha, Zhuzhou, Hengyang, Datonghu in Nanxian County, Qingshuzhui in Nan County, Ninxiang, Yueyang, Yiyang, Liuyang, Loudi. ***Jiangsu***: Yixing, Wujiang, Lianyungang, Changzhou, Xuzhou, Kunshan, Zhenjiang, Changshu, Zhangjiagang, Nantong, Wuyao in Rugao County. ***Jiangxi***: Jiujiang, Jingdezhen, Nanchang city, Shangrao, Xinjiang, Nanchang County, Yongxiu. ***Liaoning***: Shenyang. ***Ningxia***:Yinchuan. ***Shandong***: Liaocheng, Heze, Yantai, Weihai, Penglai.
Shaanxi: Xi'an. ***Shanxi***: Taiyuan, Datong, Fenyang. ***Sichuan***: Pingwu, Jiangyou, Guangyuan, Suining, Huage in Nanbu County, Jiangxing in Nanbu County, Mianyang, Jiange, Yupai in Anxian, Pixian. ***Xinjiang***: Wulumuqi.***Yunanan***: Kunming. ***Zhejiang***: Haiyan, Deqing, Pinghu, Wuyi, Yiwu, Lin'an, Suxi, Keqiao, Leqing.

2. City list according to the second measure of city sizes

Mega-cities: Beijing, Shanghai, Guangzhou, Shenzhen

Large cities: Chongqin, Xiamen, Fushan, Wuhan, Nanjing and Suzhou, Shengyang and Dalian, Jinan and Qingdao, Chengdu, Xi'an, Tianjin, Hangzhou, Ningbo, and Wenzhou.

Medium-large Cities: Hefei, Quanzhou, Zhuhai, Shantou, and Dongguan, Nanning, Shijiazhuang, Zhenzhou, Changsha, Yinchuan, Wuxi, Changzhou, Zhenjiang, Yangzhou, Nantong, Shaoxing, Huzhou, Yantai, Wulumuqi, Taiyuan, Kunming, Nanchang.

Other cities: the rest of cities not in the first three categories

3. City list according to the third measure of city sizes

Megacities (population over 10 million): Beijing, Shanghai, Guangzhou, Shenzhen, Chongqing, Tianjin.

Large cities (population in 3–10 million): Hefei, Xiamen, Fushan, Shantou, Dongguan, Zhanjiang, Nanning, Shijiazhuang, Zhenzhou, Wuhan, Changsha, Shengyang and Dalian, Suzhou, Nanjing, Wuxi, Changzhou, Xuzhou, Xi'an, Jinan, Qingdao, Taiyuan, Chengdu, Wulumiqi, Kunming, Hangzhou, Ningbo, and Wenzhou.

Medium-large cities (population in 1–3 million): Huainan, Huaibei, Fuyang, Quanzhou, Tianshui, Zhuhai, Zhongshan, Maoming, Huizhou, Yulin, Anyang, Pingdingshan, Luoyang, Jingzhou, Shashai, Yiyang, Hengyang, Yueyang, Zhuzhou, Yinchuan, Zhenjiang, Yangzhou, Nantong, Lianyungang, Nanchang, Yantai, Heze, Datong, Suining, Mianyang, Huzhou, Jiaxing.

Other cities: the rest of cities not in the first three categories

4. City list according to the fourth measure of city sizes

Different from the third measure in that: 4 cities which are *other cities* in the third measure are defined as *medium-large cities* in the fourth measure.

Appendix B: Occupation Definitions

(1) Self-employed small business owner: owns a small business that requires investment and self-employment, such as a small restaurant or a tailor's shop, etc.
(2) Professional and technician: engineers, electrical designers, software designers, interior designers, quality supervisors, and doctors. These occupations generally require formal education.
(3) Managerial staff: division manager and senior white-collar workers.
(4) General staff: ordinary clerks engaged in enterprises and institutions.

(5) Sales personnel: professional sales personnel without fixed place (such as real estate sales personnel, pharmaceutical sales personnel [excluding the pharmacy staff included in category (7)], electrical or other equipment sales personnel such as elevator sales personnel [excluding the store sales staff included in category (7)].
(6) Manufacturing worker: ordinary manufacturing industry workers.
(7) Commercial worker: includes sales staff or tally clerks in supermarkets, department stores, drug stores, computer stores, and so on.
(8) Service worker: catering industry workers and household service workers (excluding chefs), including waiters, pantry workers, and household cleaners.
(9) Construction and decoration worker: masons, carpenters, painters, plumbers, and aluminum workers, excluding the non-technical workers included in category (11).
(10) Craftsmen: tailors, cooks, drivers, machine workers, turners, fitters, nurses, kindergarten teachers, mechanics, technicians, and so on.
(11) Other occupations: waste collection, unskilled construction workers, and other workers.

References

Abdel-Rahman H, Fujita M (1990) Product varieties, marshallian externalities and city size. J Reg Sci 2:165–183

Ades A, Glaeser E (1995) Trade and circuses: explaining urban giants. Q J Econ 110:195–227

Au CC, Henderson JV (2006a) Are Chinese cities too small? Rev Econ Stud 73(3):549–576

Au CC, Henderson JV (2006b) How migration restrictions limit agglomeration and productivity in China. J Dev Econ 80:350–388

Baum-Snow N, Pavan R (2011) Understanding the city size wage gap. Working Paper. http://www.econ.brown.edu/fac/nathaniel_baum-snow/citysize_wagegap.pdf

Becker R, Henderson JV (2000) Intra-industry specialization and urban development. In: Huriot J, Thisse J (eds) Economics of cities: theoretical perspectives. Cambridge University Press, Cambridge, UK

Black D, Henderson JV (1999) A theory of urban growth. J Polit Econ 107:252–284

BMSB (Beijing Municipal Statistics Bureau 2010) Beijing Statistical Yearbook 2011, Beijing

Caplin A, Leahy J (1998) Miracle on sixth avenue. Econ J 108:62–74

Combes P, Sylvie D, Li S (2012) Urbanization and agglomeration economies in China. Working paper, presented in international workshop on regional, urban, and spatial economics, Guangzhou, China

Curran LB, Wolman H, Hill EW, Furdell K (2006) Economic wellbeing and where we live: accounting for geographical cost-of-living differences in the US. Urban Stud 43(13):2443–2466

Davis JC, Henderson JV (2003) Evidence on the political economy of the urbanization process. J Urban Econ 53:98–125

Dixit A, Stigliz JE (1977) Monopolistic competition and optimum product diversity. Am Econ Rev 67:297–308

Duranton G, Puga D (2001) Nursery cities. Am Econ Rev 91:1454–1463

Fujita M (1989) Urban economic theory: land use and city size. Cambridge University Press, New York

Fujita M, Ogawa H (1982) Multiple equilibria and structural transition of non-monocentric urban configurations. Reg Sci Urban Econ 12:161–196

Fujita M, Krugman P, Venables AJ (1999) The spatial economy. MIT Press, Cambridge, MA

Helpman E (1997) The Size of Region. In: Pines D, Sadka E, Zilcha I (eds) Topics in Public Economics. Theory and Applied Analysis, Cambridge University Press, Cambridge

Helsley R, Strange W (1990) Matching and agglomeration economies in a system of cities. J Urban Econ 20:189–212

Henderson JV (1988) Urban development: theory, fact and illusion. Oxford University Press

Henderson JV (1974) The size and types of cities. Am Econ Rev 64:640–656

Henderson JV (2002) Urbanization in developing countries. World Bank Res Obs 17:89–111

Henderson JV, Becker R (2000) Political economy of city size and formation. J Urban Econ 48:453–484

Henderson JV, Kuncoro A (1996) Industrial centralization in Indonesia. World Bank Econ Rev 10:513–540

Krugman P (1991) Increasing returns and economic geography. J Polit Econ 99(3):483–499

Lewis WA (1954) Economic development with unlimited supply of labor. Manch Sch 5:139–191

Lucas RE (2004) Life earnings and rural-urban migration. J Polit Econ 112:29–57

Moomaw R, Shatter A (1996) Urbanization and economic development: a bias toward large cities? J Urban Econ 40:13–37

Moulton B (1995) Inter-area indexes of the cost of shelter using hedonic quality adjustment techniques. J Econ 68(1):181–204

Muth R (1969) Cities and housing. University of Chicago press, Chicago

NBS (National Statistics Bureau of China 2011a) "Sixth National Census in 2010", Beijing

NBS (National Statistics Bureau of China 2011b) "China Statistical Yearbook, 2011", Beijing

NBS (National Statistics Bureau of China 2012) "A Survey Report of Peasant Workers in China, 2011", Beijing

Renaud B (1981) National urbanization policy in developing countries. Oxford University Press

Richardson H (1987) The cost of urbanization: a four country comparison. Econ Dev Cult Change 31:561–580

Roback J (1982) Wages, rents, and the quality of life. J Polit Econ 90(6):1257–1278

Rousseau MP (1995) Les Parisiens sont surproductifs. Etudes Foncieres 68:13–18

Thomas V (1980) Spatial differences in the cost of living. J Urban Econ 8:108–122

Xing C (2008) Income difference between peasant workers and urban resident workers. Manag World 5 (in Chinese)

Zheng XP (2001) Determinants of agglomeration economies and diseconomies: empirical evidence from Tokyo. Socio-Econ Plan Sci 35:131–144

Chapter 3
Dynastic Cycles and Nomadic Conquests: Further Evidence from China and World History

Qiang Chen

Abstract Conflict between nomadic and agricultural people has been a recurring phenomenon throughout world history. A recent study finds that dynastic cycles are an important determinant of nomadic conquests in the context of Sino-nomadic conflict, where an aging Chinese dynasty was more likely to be conquered. This paper extends this result in two dimensions using a sample of nomads in or near China and a sample from world history. The effects of dynastic cycles on nomadic conquests remain significant in a much broader context. Overall, the dynastic cycle appears to be a general force shaping world history that has been hitherto underappreciated.

Keywords Dynastic cycles · Nomadic conquests · Climate shocks

3.1 Introduction

Conflict between nomadic and agricultural people was a recurring phenomenon throughout the ancient world that has helped shape world history. As noted by Wells (2006 [1922], p. 70), "It was inevitable that as the two sorts of life, the agricultural and the nomadic, differentiated, a certain amount of looting and trading should develop between the two." While nomadic conquests have long captured the imaginations of leading historians (e.g., Barfield 1989, 1993; Cosmo 2002; Grousset 1970; Huntington 1907; Lattimore 1989 [1940]; Morris 2010; Toynbee 1972), the quantitative study of nomadic conflict and its outcomes has just begun in recent years. In a seminal contribution, Bai and Kung (2011) focus on the effects of climate shocks on Sino-nomadic conflict over the past two millennia. They find that nomadic incursions into settled Han Chinese regions were positively correlated with less rainfall (proxied by droughts, which drove pastoral nomads to attack the agrarian Chinese for survival) and negatively correlated with more rainfall (proxied by floods). Zhao (2012) reports similar results using different data sources.

However, climate shocks by themselves were not the only drivers of nomadic conquests. Clearly, the frequency of nomadic attack differed from the outcome because the latter also depended on the relative strengths of pastoral and sedentary peo-

T. Kinugasa et al., *Economic Growth and Transition of Industrial Structure in East Asia*, Kobe University Social Science Research Series,
https://doi.org/10.1007/978-981-13-2868-8_3

ple, which are linked to their relative positions in dynastic cycles. Therefore, Chen (2015) introduces dynastic cycles as an additional key factor shaping the outcome of Sino-nomadic conflict. By using both a dyadic approach (China vs. nomad dynastic pairs) and a time-series decadal approach, Chen (2015) shows that the likelihood of nomadic conquest increased with less rainfall, as proxied by droughts, and the number of years since a Chinese dynasty was established (which was thus weaker, on average) relative to a rival nomadic regime.

It is well known that dynastic cycles were a salient feature of Chinese history. By the standards of medieval Europe, average dynastic longevity in ancient China was short, and a major Chinese dynasty typically lasted no longer than 300 years. According to the dynastic cycle hypothesis, all historical regimes had life cycles of rises and falls and inevitably declined over time (Spengler 1926; Toynbee 1972; Olson 1986; Kennedy 1987). Consequently, the power of a dynasty was, on average, declining over time, and an aging China was more likely to be conquered by a rising nomadic power.

A variety of mechanisms have been proposed to explain the causes of dynastic cycles mostly in the context of Chinese history, such as the degeneration of royal families (Fairbank and Reischauer 1989), the Malthusian effects of population growth leading to declining cultivated land per capita (Usher 1989; Chu and Lee 1994), and tax evasion by the gentry resulting in growing vested interests (Lattimore 1989; Fairbank and Goldman 2006, p. 48).[1] The question of which mechanism is most prominent is still unsettled in the literature. Nevertheless, we can still test an implication of dynastic cycles, i.e., as agricultural dynasties age, they become increasingly likely to be conquered by younger nomadic regimes.

A natural question is whether the effects of dynastic cycles are unique to Sino-nomadic conflict or whether they hold in a much broader context. To this end, this paper extends Chen's (2015) study in two directions. First, I use a sample of nomads in or near China to examine whether the effect of dynastic cycles on conquests remains valid among nomads (i.e., nomad vs. nomad). Second, I assemble a sample from world history to explore the effect of dynastic cycles on nomadic conquests outside of China. Both samples show significant and robust effects of dynastic cycles on nomadic conquests. Therefore, dynastic cycles appear to be a general force shaping interstate conflict in the ancient world and may hold a key to understanding world history that has hitherto been underappreciated.

The rest of the paper is organized as follows. Section 3.2 presents the results of conquests among nomads in or near China. Section 3.3 presents the results of nomadic conquests from world history. Section 3.4 concludes.

[1]For a detailed review of causal mechanisms of dynastic cycles, see Chen (2015).

3.2 Conquests Among Nomads in or Near China

In this section, I examine the role of dynastic cycles in conquests among nomads in or near China. In fact, nomadic people near China not only attacked sedentary Chinese but also fought among themselves for survival and military advantage. Hence, it is interesting to determine whether the effects of dynastic cycles also occurred among nomads themselves.

The benchmark model is specified as follows:

$$conquered_i = \beta_0 + \beta_1 diff_i + \beta_2 drought_i + \beta_3 flood_i + \beta_4 levee_i + \varepsilon_i, \quad (3.1)$$

where *conquered* is a dummy variable indicating whether an older nomadic regime was conquered by a coexisting younger nomadic regime, and the subscript i refers to the ith dynastic dyad (older nomad vs. younger nomad). The key explanatory variable *diff* captures the dynastic cycle effect and is the difference between the founding year of a younger nomadic regime and that of an older nomadic regime. All dynastic data, including the founding and ending years of the nomadic regimes and their conquests, are taken from Bai (1999), a multivolume, comprehensive general history book on China.

Following Bai and Kung (2011), the climate variables are defined as "decadal share of years with recorded drought disasters in north China" (*drought*), "decadal share of years with recorded flood disasters in north China" (*flood*), and "decadal share of years with a levee breach or flooding of the Yellow river" (*levee*), which are all averaged over the period when the two nomadic regimes in question coexisted. The data for *drought* and *flood* are derived from Zhang et al. (1994) and Chen (1939), while the data for *levee* are drawn from the Editorial Committee of the Irrigation History of the Yellow River (1982).[2]

Table 3.1 presents data related to conquests among nomadic regimes in or near China. There were 22 dyads of nomadic rivals with 7 realized conquests: the Former Zhao was conquered by the Later Zhao, the Former Yan was conquered by the Former Qin, the Former Qin was conquered by the Later Qin, the Northern Qi was conquered by the Northern Zhou, the Liao was conquered by the Jin, and the Western Xia and the Jin were both conquered by the Yuan.

Because the dependent variable *conquered* is a dummy variable, it is a common practice to estimate a probit or logit model. Alternatively, it can be estimated by OLS, i.e., a linear probability model, as a convenient benchmark. The estimation results are presented in Table 3.2.

Columns (1), (2) and (3) of Table 3.2 report the results of OLS, probit and logit estimations, respectively, while column (4) reports the marginal effects of the logit estimation. In all estimations, the coefficient of *diff* is positively significant at least

[2]See Chen (2015) for the details of data construction. Both Bai and Kung (2011) and Chen (2015) use additional climate variables, such as snow, frost disasters and historical temperature, which are largely insignificant in their studies. Due to the small size of current sample, I include only *drought*, *flood*, and *levee* to preserve degrees of freedom.

Table 3.1 Conquests among Nomadic Regimes in or near China

Older Nomadic Regime	Older Nomad duration	Younger Nomadic Regime	Younger Nomad duration	Difference in Regime Age (*diff*)	Older Nomad conquered
Xianbei	150–235	Wuhuan	190–207	40	0
Former Zhao	304–329	Later Zhao	319–351	15	1
Later Zhao	319–351	Former Yan	337–370	18	0
Former Yan	337–370	Former Qin	351–394	14	1
Former Qin	351–394	Later Qin	384–417	33	1
Former Qin	351–394	Later Yan	384–407	33	0
Former Qin	351–394	Northern Wei	386–534	35	0
Later Qin	384–417	Later Yan	384–407	0	0
Later Qin	384–417	Northern Wei	386–534	2	0
Later Yan	384–407	Northern Wei	386–534	2	0
East Wei	534–550	West Wei	535–556	1	0
West Wei	535–556	Northern Qi	550–577	15	0
Northern Qi	550–577	Northern Zhou	557–581	7	1
Eastern Turk	609–629	Tibet	629–877	20	0
Eastern Turk	609–629	Uighur	744–840	135	0
Tibet	629–877	Uighur	744–840	115	0
Liao	907–1125	Jin	1115–1234	208	1
Liao	907–1125	Western Xia	1038–1227	131	0
Western Xia	1038–1227	Jin	1115–1234	77	0
Western Xia	1038–1227	Yuan	1206–1368	168	1
Jin	1115–1234	Yuan	1206–1368	91	1
Eastern Mongols	1401–1636	Oirats	1401–?	0	0

Data source Bai (1999)

at the 5% level, which supports the dynastic cycle hypothesis, i.e., an older regime is weaker, on average, and thus more likely to be conquered. The marginal effect of *diff,* as shown in column (4), indicates that when an older nomadic regime was founded one year before a competing younger nomadic regime, the likelihood of the former being conquered by the latter increases by 4.46%, the magnitude of which is economically significant and much larger than the marginal effect of 1.03% estimated by Chen (2015) for the Sino-nomadic sample (China vs. nomad).[3]

The coefficient of *drought* is positively significant at least at the 10% level, whereas the coefficient for *flood* is negatively significant at least at the 5% level. These results

[3]A possible interpretation is that nomadic regimes declined at relatively faster rates on average than agricultural dynasties, since nomadic regimes were typically more personalised and less institutionalised than agricultural dynasties.

Table 3.2 Regression results for conquests among Nomadic Regimes in or near China

	(1) OLS	(2) Probit	(3) Logit	(4) Marginal effects
diff	0.00353***	0.0241**	0.0413**	0.00446***
	(0.00110)	(0.0102)	(0.0191)	(0.00152)
drought	1.181*	5.464**	9.428*	1.0186***
	(0.579)	(2.551)	(5.131)	(0.350)
flood	−2.556***	−18.30**	−31.46**	−3.396***
	(0.694)	(7.444)	(14.28)	(0.719)
levee	1.072	9.495	16.99	1.834*
	(0.803)	(6.614)	(12.18)	(0.976)
constant	0.356**	−0.145	−0.328	
	(0.164)	(0.562)	(0.986)	
N	22	22	22	22
(pseudo) R^2	0.406	0.466	0.463	0.463

Dependent variable: *conquered*
Notes Robust standard errors are in parentheses. * $p < 0.1$, ** $p < 0.05$, *** $p < 0.01$

are consistent with the findings of Bai and Kung (2011) and Chen (2015) that less rainfall disrupts the fragile nomadic equilibrium and pushes nomads into looting and warfare for survival. The coefficient of *levee*, a levee breach of the Yellow river, is largely insignificant.

In summary, while one should be cautious in interpreting the results from a small sample, the consistent positive significance of *diff* across the estimations presented in Table 3.2 suggests that the effect of dynastic cycles on nomadic conquests also holds among nomadic regimes and not just between agricultural dynasties and nomadic regimes.

3.3 Nomadic Conquests in World History

Conflict between nomadic pastoralists and agrarian agriculturists was a common phenomenon throughout the ancient world.[4] This fact offers a unique opportunity to test the generality of the effect of dynastic cycles. Moreover, to verify external validity (Stock and Watson 2006), it is interesting to determine whether the effect of dynastic cycles on nomadic conquests remains valid outside of China.

However, the price of moving to a world sample is that we lose all the climate variables and end up with only the key variable *diff*:

[4]For example, see Wells (2006 [1922]), Bentley and Ziegler (2003, Chap. 18), Barfield (1989, 1993, 2001, 2011), and Turchin (2009) for excellent expositions.

$$conquered_i = \beta_0 + \beta_1 diff_i + \varepsilon_i, \quad (3.2)$$

where *conquered* is a dummy variable indicating whether an agricultural dynasty was conquered by a nomadic regime, and the subscript i refers to the ith dynastic dyad from the world historical sample (agricultural vs. nomadic regime). The definition of *diff* is essentially the same, i.e., the number of years that an agricultural dynasty was founded before a competing nomadic regime.

Obviously, a host of factors related to dynastic rivalry has been ignored in such a simplistic regression. However, because *diff* remains fixed after two competing regimes were founded, it is reasonable to treat *diff* as a predetermined regressor. For example, climate conditions after the founding of the dynasties presumably had no effects on *diff*, which was determined when dynasties were established. In other words, as long as omitted factors in Eq. (3.2) are not correlated with *diff*, we can still consistently estimate the coefficient of *diff*, namely, the effect of dynastic cycles.

In collecting relevant historical data, I follow a two-step procedure to avoid selection bias. First, I consult a comprehensive world history book for possible agrarian-nomadic rivalry dyads—in this case, Bentley and Ziegler's (2003) popular 1169-page *Traditions and Encounters: A Global Perspective on the Past*. Second, I consult the *Encyclopedia Britannica Online*, *Oxford Dictionary of Dates* (Beeching 1997), and other sources to determine the founding years of these regimes. It is not unusual to find that specific founding years are unavailable (especially for nomadic regimes) and cannot be included in the sample. Before proceeding, a note about the distinction between agrarian and nomadic regimes is in order. Because the goal is to study the probability of an agrarian regime being conquered by a (semi)nomadic regime, I always identify the regime that was *relatively* more agrarian than its rival as the host dynasty (the target of conquest), and no absolute standard is applied. Consequently, it is possible to classify the same regime as both agrarian and nomadic in different observed dyads. For example, the Sasanid Empire in the Middle East is treated as a nomadic regime when it is paired with the Roman Empire, but it is treated as an agrarian regime when it is paired with the Arab Empire because the latter was clearly more nomadic than the former. The data are presented in Table 3.3, and Appendix provides a historical narrative and the data sources.

The estimation results are presented in Table 3.4. Columns (1), (2) and (3) of Table 3.4 report the results of OLS, probit and logit estimations, respectively, while column (4) reports the marginal effects from the logit estimation. Regardless of the estimation method, the coefficient of *diff* is positively significant at least at the 5% level, which supports the dynastic cycle hypothesis, i.e., an aging agricultural dynasty is more prone to being conquered by a rival nomadic regime. The marginal effect of *diff*, as shown in column (4), indicates that when an agricultural dynasty was founded one year before a competing nomadic regime, the likelihood of the former being conquered by the latter increases by 0.941%, which is close to the marginal effect of 1.03% estimated by Chen (2015) for the Sino-nomadic sample (China vs. nomad).

While one should again be cautious in interpreting the results from a small sample, the fact that the dynastic cycles variable (*diff*) is positively significant for nomadic

Table 3.3 Data from world history, excluding China

Host dynasty	Host founding	Nomadic Regime	Nomadic founding	Years founded earlier	Host conquered
26th Dynasty (Egypt)	−685	Achaemenid	−558	127	1
Mermnad (Lydia)	−680	Achaemenid	−558	122	1
New Babylonia Empire	−626	Achaemenid	−558	68	1
Macedon	−359	Achaemenid	−558	−199	0
Roman Empire	−27	Parthia	−247	−220	0
Roman Empire	−27	Sasanid	224	251	0
Roman Empire	−27	Visigoth	395	422	1
Eastern Roman Empire	395	Sasanid	224	−171	0
Eastern Roman Empire	395	Hun	432	37	0
Eastern Roman Empire	395	Vandal	439	44	0
Eastern Roman Empire	395	Ostrogoth	454	59	0
Eastern Roman Empire	395	Arab Empire	622	227	0
Eastern Roman Empire	395	Umayyad	661	266	0
Eastern Roman Empire	395	Abbasid	750	355	0
Eastern Roman Empire	395	Ottoman	1299	904	1
Sasanid	224	Arab Empire	622	398	1
Visigoth	395	Umayyad	661	266	1
Merovingian (Franks)	481	Umayyad	661	180	0
Abbasid	750	Il-Khanid	1256	506	1
Kievan Rus	879	Khazar	733	−146	0
Kievan Rus	879	Golden Horde	1235	356	1
Khwarezm-Shah	1077	Mongol	1206	129	1
Ayyubid Dynasty	1173	Il-Khanid	1256	83	1
Delhi Sultanate	1211	Tamerlane	1370	159	1
Habsburg	1273	Ottoman	1299	26	0
Muscovy	1480	Khanate of the Crimea	1443	−37	0

Note See Appendix for data sources and a narrative

conquests in different samples with very different time and spatial coverage does lend support to the generality of dynastic cycles as an important determinant of state conflict outcomes in the ancient world.

Figure 3.1 provides a visual representation of the robust positive correlation between *conquered* and *diff* in different samples. The upper left panel is a scatterplot for nomad-versus-China with 47 observations and a correlation coefficient of 0.36 taken from Chen (2015). The upper right panel is a scatterplot for nomads near China with 22 observations and a correlation coefficient of 0.27. The lower left panel

Table 3.4 Regression results for conquests in world history

	(1) OLS	(2) Probit	(3) Logit	(4) Marginal Effect
diff	0.000890***	0.00302***	0.00478**	0.000941**
	(0.000218)	(0.00113)	(0.00191)	(0.000279)
constant	0.279***	−0.703**	−1.111**	
	(0.0892)	(0.300)	(0.501)	
N	26	26	26	26
(pseudo) R^2	0.187	0.160	0.155	0.155

Dependent variable: *conquered*

Notes Robust standard errors are in parentheses. * $p < 0.1$, ** $p < 0.05$, *** $p < 0.01$

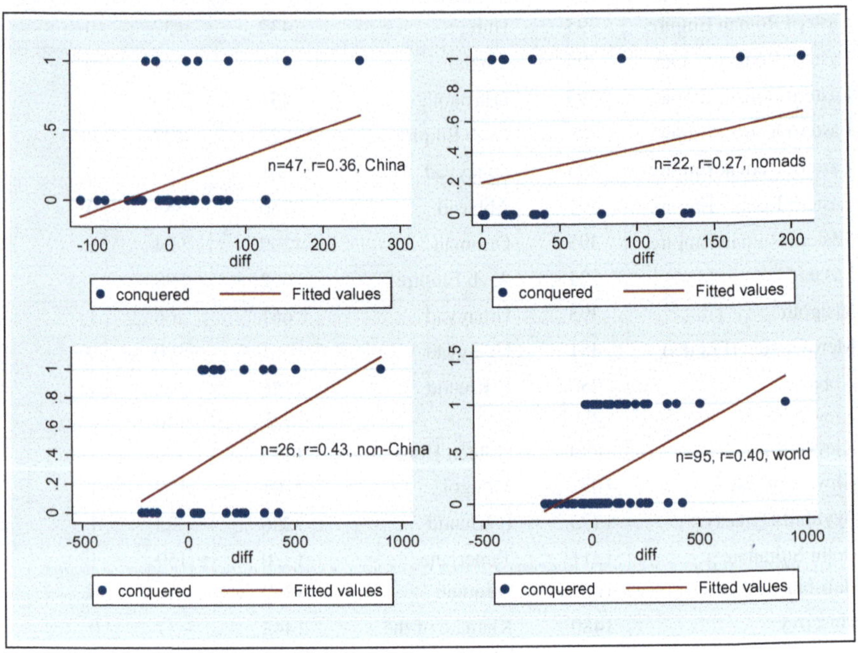

Fig. 3.1 The correlation between *conquered* and *diff* in different samples

is a scatterplot for the world history sample excluding China with 26 observations and a correlation coefficient of 0.43. The lower right panel is a scatterplot for the whole world, including China, with 95 observations and a correlation coefficient of 0.40.

3.4 Conclusion

Historians have long thought that all historical regimes had life cycles of rises and falls and that regimes inevitably declined over time, an argument that has come to be known as the dynastic cycle hypothesis. A direct test of the dynastic cycle hypothesis is desirable but measuring the "power" of a dynasty over time across a long time span is difficult. Chen (2015) approaches this issue by indirectly testing a natural implication of the dynastic cycle hypothesis, i.e., that an older agricultural dynasty is weaker, on average, and thus more likely to be conquered by a younger nomadic regime. The data from Sino-nomadic conflict over the past two millennia are consistent with the dynastic cycle hypothesis.

However, is the effect of dynastic cycles specific to Chinese history or to conflict between agricultural and nomadic people or does it hold in a more general context? Using a sample of nomads in or near China, this study shows that the effect of dynastic cycles holds among nomadic regimes, i.e., an older nomadic regime is more likely to be conquered by a younger nomadic regime. Moreover, using a sample from world history, this study further demonstrates that the effect of dynastic cycles is also valid in the ancient world outside of China.

Overall, this study has greatly expanded the applicability of the dynastic cycle hypothesis to the ancient world and beyond the epic struggle between nomadic and agricultural people. It appears that the inexorable law of dynastic rise and fall is a general force shaping the outcome of interstate conflict throughout the ancient world, which may hold a key to understanding world history that has been underappreciated until now.

Acknowledgements I thank Zhiwu Chen, Xiuqi Fang, and seminar participants at the Third International Symposium of Quantitative History (Peking University), and a referee for insightful comments. I am grateful for financial supports from National Science Foundation of China (NSFC 71473149).

Appendix: Data from World History

In 685 BCE, the Twenty-sixth Dynasty of Egypt was established. It lasted until 525 BCE,[5] when it was conquered by the Achaemenid Empire, which was founded in 558 BCE by Cyrus the Great, who declared himself the king of both Persia and Media.[6] In 680 BCE, Gyges established the Mermnad dynasty of Lydia in western Anatolia,[7] which was conquered by the Achaemenid Empire in 546 BCE.[8] In 626

[5]Dodson and Hilton (2004).

[6]Bentley and Ziegler (2003), p. 162.

[7]"Gyges." Encyclopedia Britannica Online. Encyclopedia Britannica Inc., 2011. Web. 11 Nov. 2011.

[8]Bentley and Ziegler (2003), p. 168.

BCE, Nabopolassar was recognized as king and began the New Babylonian Empire,[9] which dominated Mesopotamia for over half a century until being conquered by the Achaemenid Empire in 539 BCE.[10] The kingdom of Macedon was founded when King Philip II came to power in 359 BCE and built a powerful military that overcame traditional clans and made him the ruler of Macedon.[11] Under Alexander the Great, Macedon wiped out the Achaemenid Empire in 330 BCE.[12]

The Roman Empire was founded in 27 BCE when Octavian became Augustus,[13] and it suffered a series of nomadic attacks as it aged. As an older enemy from the Middle East, the Parthian Empire was founded in 247 BCE and did not gain the upper hand fighting the Roman Empire.[14] When the Sasanid Empire replaced the Parthian Empire in 224,[15] it also inherited its predecessor's hostility toward the Roman Empire and its successor, the Eastern Roman Empire, but no conquest occurred. In its later years, the Roman Empire faced increasing pressure from various Germanic tribes moving to its north border. In 395, the Roman Empire was split in half,[16] marking the beginning of the Eastern Roman Empire or the Byzantine Empire.[17] The Visigothic kingdom was founded in 395 when Alaric I became its king and famously led the Visigoths to sack Rome in 410,[18] but the (Western) Roman Empire lingered until 476.

The Hunnic Empire was founded in 432 when king Rugila unified the Huns into a cohesive group[19] and posed a great threat to the Eastern Roman Empire, especially when Attila was in power. In 439, King Gaiseric of the Vandals threw off Roman overlordship and established an independent autocracy in North Africa, which was later conquered by the Eastern Roman Empire in 533.[20] Another Gothic group, the

---

[9]Grayson (1975).

[10]Bentley and Ziegler (2003), p. 162.

[11]Bentley and Ziegler (2003), p. 250.

[12]Bentley and Ziegler (2003), p. 251.

[13]Bentley and Ziegler (2003), p. 278.

[14]Bentley and Ziegler (2003), p. 166.

[15]Beeching (1997), p.277.

[16]Beeching (1997), p.279.

[17]I treat the Roman Empire and the Western Roman Empire as one empire because the latter certainly inherited many aspects of the former, including its aging governing machinery. In contrast, the Eastern Roman Empire is treated as a new empire with distinct characteristics. For historical evidence supporting this treatment, see Bentley and Ziegler (2003), Chap. 13.

[18]"Visigoth." Encyclopedia Britannica Online. Encyclopedia Britannica Inc., 2011. Web. 11 Nov. 2011. Although Rome was sacked again by the Vandals in 455 and the Roman Empire was not officially ended until 476, I treat it as conquered by the Visigoths (the regression results are robust to this treatment).

[19]"Hun." Encyclopedia Britannica Online. Encyclopedia Britannica Inc., 2011. Web. 11 Nov. 2011.

[20]"Vandals." Encyclopedia Britannica Online. Encyclopedia Britannica Inc., 2011. Web. 11 Nov. 2011.

Ostrogoths, gained independence when it broke away from Hunnic control in the battle of Nedao in 454.[21] and later became a rival of the Eastern Roman Empire.

The Arab Empire was founded in 622 when the prophet Muhammad fled Mecca to Medina and organized his followers into a cohesive community.[22] The Arab Empire toppled the Sasanid dynasty in 651 and posed a threat to the Eastern Roman Empire. The Umayyad dynasty, the first of the two great dynasties of the Muslim Empire of the Caliphate, was established in 661 when Muawiyah established himself as the first Umayyad caliph following the first Muslim civil war.[23] In 711, the Umayyad dynasty destroyed the Visigoths and conquered most of the Iberian peninsula.[24] The Abbasid Dynasty, the second of the two great dynasties of the Muslim Empire of the Caliphate, was established in 750[25] and competed with the Eastern Roman Empire. The lethal foe of the Eastern Roman Empire came from Asia Minor at a much later time. Founded in 1299,[26] the Ottoman Empire conquered Constantinople in 1453 and formally ended the Eastern Roman Empire.[27]

The Merovingian dynasty was established when Clovis became the ruler of the Franks in 481. In 732 at the battle of Tours (the central part of France), the Merovingian dynasty turned back a Muslim army that had ventured from Spain.[28]

The Kievan Rus was established by the Viking Oleg around 879.[29] After its founding, the Kievan Rus endured various nomadic attacks, most notably from the Khazars, the Pechenegs, the Kipchak-Cuman confederation,[30] and the Mongols. The Khazar empire was founded in 737 when the Khazars established their capital at Itil (located near the mouth of the Volga River) and accepted the Caucasus Mountains as their southern boundary. By the 10th century, the Khazars had an uneasy relation with the Kievan Rus and were crushed in 965.[31] The Mongol Empire was founded in 1206 when Genghis Khan was proclaimed khan within the All Mongols league.[32] In 1235, the Golden Horde (Khanate of Kipchak) was founded when Batu, Genghis Khan's

[21]" Gepidae." and "Hun." Encyclopedia Britannica Online. Encyclopedia Britannica Inc., 2011. Web. 11 Nov. 2011.

[22]Bentley and Ziegler (2003), p. 359.

[23]"Umayyad Dynasty." Encyclopedia Britannica Online. Encyclopedia Britannica Inc., 2011. Web. 13 Nov. 2011.

[24]Bentley and Ziegler (2003), p. 363.

[25]"Abbasid Dynasty." Encyclopedia Britannica Online. Encyclopedia Britannica, 2011. Web. 11 Nov. 2011.

[26]Ackermann (2008), vol. 2, p. Chronology, xxv.

[27]Beeching (1997), p. 291.

[28]Bentley and Ziegler (2003), pp. 444–445.

[29]"Kievan Rus." Encyclopedia Britannica Online. Encyclopedia Britannica Inc., 2011. Web. 11 Nov. 2011.

[30]I do not include the Pechenegs and the Kipchak-Cumen confederation in the sample because their founding years are unclear.

[31]"Khazar." Encyclopedia Britannica Online. Encyclopedia Britannica Inc., 2011. Web. 11 Nov. 2011.

[32]"Mongol." Encyclopedia Britannica Online. Encyclopedia Britannica, 2011. Web. 11 Nov. 2011.

grandson, was elected the commander-in-chief of the western part of the Mongol Empire.[33] In 1240, the Golden Horde sacked and burned the city of Kiev.[34]

The Khwarezm-Shah Dynasty was established in 1077 and ruled in Central Asia and Iran until it was overrun by the Mongol Empire in 1231.[35] The Il-Khanid Dynasty was founded by Hulegu, a grandson of Genghis Khan, in 1256 and destroyed the Abbasid Dynasty in 1258.[36] In 1173, Saladin (Salah ad-Din) replaced the Shi'i Fatimid Caliphate in Egypt with the Sunni Muslim Ayyubid dynasty, which in 1260 fell to the invasion of the Il-Khanid Dynasty.[37]

In 1211, the Delhi Sultanate was established when Sultan Iltutmish came to power and made his permanent capital at Delhi.[38] In 1398, it was shattered by Tamerlane's empire, which was founded in 1370 when Tamerlane proclaimed himself sovereign of the Chagatai line of khans at Samarkand.[39] In 1273, Rudolf IV of Habsburg was elected the German King and established the Habsburg dynasty, which later struggled with the Ottoman Empire, founded in 1299.[40] The Khanate of the Crimea, as a successor state of the Mongol Empire, was founded in 1443 and staged occasional raids into the emergent Muscovy, which was established in 1480 when it declared independence.[41]

[33] "Batu." Encyclopedia Britannica Online. Encyclopedia Britannica Inc., 2011. Web. 12 Nov. 2011.

[34] "Golden Horde." Encyclopedia Britannica Online. Encyclopedia Britannica Inc., 2011. Web. 11 Nov. 2011.

[35] "Khwarezm-Shah Dynasty." Encyclopedia Britannica Online. Encyclopedia Britannica Inc., 2011. Web. 11 Nov. 2011

[36] "Il-Khanid Dynasty." Encyclopedia Britannica Online. Encyclopedia Britannica, 2011. Web. 12 Nov. 2011.

[37] "Ayyubid dynasty." Encyclopedia Britannica Online. Encyclopedia Britannica Inc., 2011. Web. 11 Nov. 2011.

[38] "Delhi sultanate." Encyclopedia Britannica Online. Encyclopedia Britannica Inc., 2011. Web. 12 Nov. 2011.

[39] "Timur." Encyclopedia Britannica Online. Encyclopedia Britannica Inc., 2011. Web. 12 Nov. 2011.

[40] "House of Habsburg." Encyclopedia Britannica Online. Encyclopedia Britannica Inc., 2011. Web. 12 Nov. 2011.

[41] "Khanate of the Crimea." Encyclopedia Britannica Online. Encyclopedia Britannica Inc., 2011. Web. 11 Nov. 2011.

References

Ackermann M, Schroeder M, Terry J, Upshur J, Whitters M (eds) (2008) Encyclopedia of world history. Facts on File, New York

Bai S (1999) Zhongguo tongshi (A general history of China). Shanghai Renmin Chubanshe, Shanghai

Bai Y, Kung JK (2011) Climate shocks and Sino-nomadic conflict. Rev Econ Stat 93:970–981

Barfield TJ (1989) The perilous frontier: Nomadic empires and China. Blackwell, Oxford

Barfield TJ (1993) The nomadic alternative. Prentice Hall, Upper Saddle River, NJ

Barfield TJ (2001) The shadow empires: imperial state formation along the Chinese-nomad frontier. In: Alcock et. al. (ed) Empires. Cambridge University Press, Cambridge

Barfield TJ (2011) Nomadic pastoralism. In: Bentley J (ed) Oxford handbook of world history, Chapter 9. Oxford University Press, Oxford

Beeching CL (1997) Oxford dictionary of dates, 2nd edn. Oxford University Press, Oxford

Bentley JH, Ziegler HF (2003) Traditions and encounters: a global perspective on the past. McGraw-Hill, New York

Chen G (1939) Zhongguo lidai tianzai renhuo biao (historical tabulation of natural and man-made disasters in China). Shanghai Shudian, Shanghai

Chen Q (2015) Climate shocks, dynastic cycles, and nomadic conquests: evidence from historical China. Oxford Econ Papers 67:185–204

Chu CYC, Lee RD (1994) Famine, revolt, and the dynastic cycle: population dynamics in historic China. J of Pop Econ 7:351–378

Cosmo ND (2002) Ancient China and its enemies: the rise of nomadic power in East Asian history. Cambridge University Press, Cambridge

Dodson A, Hilton D (2004) The complete royal families of ancient Egypt. The American University in Cairo Press, London

Editorial Committee of the Irrigation History of the Yellow River (1982). Huanghe shuili shi shuyao (A concise narrative of irrigation history of the Yellow River). Zhongguo Shuili Chubanshe, Beijing

Fairbank JK, Goldman M (2006) China: a new history, 2nd, enlarged edn. Harvard University Press, Cambridge

Fairbank JK, Reischauer EO (1989) China: tradition and transformation, revised edn. Houghton Mifflin Harcourt, Boston

Grayson AK (1975) Assyrian and Babylonian chronicles. J. J, Augustin, Locust Valley, NY

Grousset R (1970) The empire of the steppes: a history of Central Asia. Rutgers University Press, Piscataway, NJ

Huntington E (1907) The pulse of Asia: a journey in Central Asia illustrating the geographic basis of history. Houghton Mifflin, Boston

Kennedy P (1987) The rise and fall of great powers. Random House, New York

Lattimore O (1989 [1940]) The inner Asian frontier of China. Oxford University Press, New York

Morris I (2010) Why the West rules—for now. Farrar, Strauss and Giroux, New York

Olson M (1986) The rise and decline of nations. Yale University Press, New Haven

Spengler O (1926) The decline of the West. Allen and Unwin, London

Stock J, Watson M (2006) Introduction to econometrics. Addison-Wesley, Boston

Toynbee AJ (1972) A study of history, revised and abridged. Oxford University Press, London

Turchin P (2009) A theory for formation of large empires. J of Global Hist 4:191–217

Usher D (1989) The dynastic cycle and the stationary state. Am Econ Rev 79:1031–1044

Wells HG (2006 [1922]) A short history of the world. Penguin Group, London

Zhang B, Feng F, Zhang L, Li H (1994) Zhongguo nongye ziran zaihai shiliao ji (A compendium of historical materials on the natural disasters in Chinese agriculture). Shaaxi Kexue Jishu Chubanshe, Xi'an, China

Zhao H (2012) Qihou bianhua shifou yingxiang le woguo guoqu liangqianqianjian de nongye shehui wending? (Did climate change affect the social stability of Chinese agrarian economy in the past 2000 years?) Jingjixue Jikan (China Economic Quarterly) 11:691–722

Chapter 4
International Value, International Production Price and Unequal Exchange

Zhixuan Feng

Abstract This article reviews the critiques on Emmanuel's unequal exchange theory, and finds that a crucial concept, international value, has been neglect. Considering international value, there is no relationship between the formation of international production price that is the foundation of unequal exchange and the perfect mobility of capital among countries. An empirical estimation of equalization of profit rate based on the framework of regulation capital is used to certify this viewpoint. By introducing international value, the unequal exchange theory can survive from the critique focusing on the reality of international profit rate equalization. However, the international concept also implies that unequal exchange is not a straight result of the difference of domestic income distribution between countries, but a consequence of the international division of labor. The author also examines the existence of unequal exchange by calculating the gap between international production price and international value, i.e. the volume of transferred value of 40 countries, and finds that unequal exchange does exist and is significant enough to affect the development of one country.

Keywords Unequal exchange · International value
International production price · Equalization of profit rate

4.1 Introduction

Unequal exchange theory put forward by Emmanuel (1972) was very famous and caused a great debate in 1970 and 1980s, but not very attractive today. Emmanuel's theory has two basic points. First, he argues that the international production price has regulated the world market since there is unlimited capital mobility and every regional profit rate had equalized in the international level. Therefore, the country whose production price is lower than its value suffers from value outflow and vice versa. Second, the underdevelopment countries have lower wages, and so that their production price is lower than value. Emmanuel treats wage as an exogenous variable

T. Kinugasa et al., *Economic Growth and Transition of Industrial Structure in East Asia*, Kobe University Social Science Research Series,
https://doi.org/10.1007/978-981-13-2868-8_4

and thinks that the wage level can explain the uneven development between cores and peripheries.

Such a theory caused many critiques. The main critiques can be divided into three kinds. The first kind is related to this theory's foundation: international production price. Some scholars argue that international production price could not have been formed. Equalized profit rate means free capital movement, and production price lower than value comes from overinvestment and overproduction in certain area or industry. Nevertheless, if overinvestment has occurred, the area must have enjoyed great capital accumulation, thus underdevelopment also must have disappeared. However, the fact is, most peripheries are troubled by the lack of capital and investment. So international production price and unequal exchange are not real (De Janvry and Kramer 1979; Chandra 1986; Houston and Paus 1987; Birkan 2015).

The second kind is mainly on Emmanuel's misunderstanding of wage. Wage cannot be regarded as an exogenous variable. It is determined by capital accumulation. Moreover, it is not lower wage straightly relevant to value outflow, but a higher rate of surplus value is. Considering productivity, lower wage might coexist with a higher value of labor force and lower surplus value rate. Because surplus value rate is determined by the ratio of the necessary labor time to surplus labor time, considering two countries, one country's workers have higher real wages, in another word, their value of labor force contains more use values. If the labor productivity of this country is high enough, the workers can produce these use values in a shorter time. Given the same working day, the surplus value rate is higher in this country, although its real wage is also higher than the other country (Horward and King 2014; Houston and Paus 1987; Birkan 2015).

The last kind of critiques focus on Emmanuel's assumption of the complete division of labor in the world market. Many formal models have demonstrated that there is no certain relationship between the direction of value transfer and real wage level under the condition of the incomplete division of labor. The real world is, of course, a system of incomplete division of labor, so Emmanuel's theory does not hold up (Gibson 1980; Liossatos 1980).

To be honest, these critiques have a fatal influence on unequal exchange theory and the followers of this theory did not offer response powerful enough. So as a result, the attention on this theory has decreased since the 1990s and unequal exchange is not regarded as a crucial phenomenon in the capitalist world system. However, as shown below, these critiques are not all hitting the point, and although unequal exchange theory does have some problem, it is still a powerful explanation of the divergence of economic development between developed countries and developing countries. The purpose of this article is to review the critiques and reconstruct the framework of unequal exchange by bringing back the concept of international value.

4.2 International Value, International Production Price and Equalization of Profit Rate

4.2.1 The Lost Concept: International Value

In the debate on the unequal exchange theory, the first critique is regarded as the most serious one, since the second and third critiques are just offering some possible situation in which Unequal exchange is not true, while the first shows us a necessary contradiction between unequal exchange theory and the real world. However, this critique is only substituting one kind of misunderstanding of international production price by another kind of misunderstanding. For either the critics or the followers of unequal exchange, the perfect mobility of capital among countries is the necessary condition of the formation of international production price, but it is not true.

In my opinion, to Emmanuel and most critics, there is a crucial but forgotten category, that is, international value. In Marx's approach to value theory, individual value or individual labor time should first be integrated into value or socially necessary labor time, and then value could be transformed to production price. This logic should also hold in the world market, although one's individual labor time has been integrated into a unique value at the domestic level, but it is still individual value in the international level. Therefore, the approach should have been that national values were integrated into international value and then the international value was transformed to production price. However, in the debate of unequal exchange, most scholars neglect this and discuss the value transformation at the national level.

If we accept this approach, then unequal exchange could be understood in a totally different way. If we called value transfer in exchange as unequal exchange, then there are at least three kinds of unequal exchange. The first one is caused by the difference between international value and national value, which is mainly relevant to the gap of productivity. Mandel (1975) argue that this kind of unequal exchange is important in international trade in his famous book *late capitalism*. This point of view worth further studying, but for the purpose of this paper, I am not focusing on it. The second one results from the deviation between international production price and international value; there are also some factors like the monopoly that could cause international market price deviates from international production price, so this deviation is the third kind of unequal exchange. Emmanuel's theory using value transformation to prove the existence of unequal exchange, so his theory should have been located at the second kind of the unequal exchange. Nonetheless, both Emmanuel himself and the critics didn't notice this. As we are focusing on Emmanuel's unequal exchange theory, we will only discuss the second kind of unequal exchange, and for the left part of this paper, the word "unequal exchange" refers to this kind of unequal exchange.

As we introduce the category of international value, we should review the criticisms again. First, we find that unequal exchange theory could survive under critique 1. Both Emmanuel and Critics use the equalization of regional profit rate as the foundation of international production price, but actually, the international production price is transformed from international value, and international value is an industrial category, not a regional one. As productivity vary from country to country, national values in countries are different too, so are the profit rates. And after international value transformed into international production price, nothing would change. This logic is totally following Marx's approach. Thinking about the equalization of domestic profit rate, it is the equalization of average industrial profit rate, not average regional profit rate. The same as the domestic production price, international production price only need free capital mobility between industries, that is to say, although capital cannot flow from one country to another country, if it could flow from one industry to another industry within one country, the mobility of capital between industries still holds at the international level.

Further, profit rate equalization is a process between industries, and this process coexists with the varieties of productivity, wage rate among enterprises within one industry. And in the international market, in a certain industry, there are also different productivities, wage rates and other factors that have influences on profit rate between countries, and these varieties are not contradict to equalization of profit rate in the international level. If profit rates of different industries equalized, the average profit rates of countries cannot reach to a same level, because some countries' productivities are lower, or their rates of surplus value are higher than average level in most industries and so the average profit rate is lower than the equalized profit rate in the international market and vice versa.

Let us assume that capital cannot move freely and instantly between countries, but within every country capital can flow from one industry to another perfectly. If the trade between countries is sufficient and so that there is an international common market, it is easy to image that when one industry's average profit rate of every country is higher than other industries, in most countries, capital will flow into this industry and the output of this industry will increase. Finally, as a result that supply exceeds demand, the price declines and the average profit rate of this industry decrease correspondingly. Therefore, in such a situation, even if capital mobility is restricted, international production price can format in such a way.

Therefore, whether capital can flow across the border freely, if there is perfect mobility of capital within countries and efficient international trade, the capital as a whole is allocated among industries freely enough. And of course, the international production price can exist. So Emmanuel himself uses the perfect mobility of capital worldwide to demonstrate his theory is wrong and unnecessary, and critics just get this mistake. The only two foundations of international production price, efficient international trade and capital mobility within a certain region are commonly recognized as the reality of world market.

Although there is no equalization of profit rate between countries, the unequal exchange still holds up. After the formation of international production price, some industries' international production price is higher than international value and we call such kind of industries as value inflow industries, for they claim a bigger part of value than they produce, and correspondingly we call the industries whose international production price lower than international value as value outflow industries. If the scale of value inflow industries is large enough to make the inflow value more than outflow value outflow in a certain country, then this country benefits from unequal exchange. And in the opposite situation, the value outflow is larger and so that outflow value is more than inflow value, then the country suffers from the value transfer caused by unequal exchange.

It is clear that as there is no equalized profit rate of countries, the first critique has no meaning at all, and over-accumulation in a country has no relationship with value transfer and unequal exchange.

4.2.2 Empirical Evidence of the Formation of International Production Price

In the first part of this section, we argue that the formation of international production price is not based upon the capital mobility on an international level. Although its logic is clear and straight, we still need some empirical evidences to confirm the validity of this viewpoint. So in this part, we offer an approach to conduct it.

The most direct conclusion of our theory on international value and international production price is that the profit rates between industries are equalized but profit rates between countries are not, so we can calculate the average profit rate of every country in a certain industry and compare this industry's average profit rate with other industries' average profit rate. If they are close to each other enough, then we can say that international production price has formed. We can also calculate the average profit rate of every industry in a certain country, and compare it with other countries' average profit rate, if they are not close enough then we can confirm that international production price can be formed without the capital mobility and the equalization of profit rate among countries.

To get the profit rate of an industry in certain country, we use the method above:

$$r = \frac{s}{(w + a)t + k} \tag{4.1}$$

r is the profit rate, and s is the volume of profit, w is the amount of advance wage and a is the amount of intermediate input, t is the turnover velocity of floating capital, and k is the fixed capital stock.

There are three main problems in calculating the average profit rate. The first one is that equalization of profit rate is realized by capital movement so only capital that is able to move is engaged in this equalization process. There is much sunk capital of backward advantage and capital of advantage and monopoly techniques in a certain industry. The former doesn't exit the industry for many reasons even if its profit rate has been very low. And the latter can have excess profit rate because other capital cannot get their techniques. So it is obvious that not all the capital participates the process of profit rate equalization.

Shaikh (2008) create a new concept "regulation capital" to describe the capital, which is mobile, and have the "normal" or "available" techniques. Only the profit rate of regulation capital is equalized. Shaikh also offers a method to calculate the regulation capital's profit rate:

$$y_t = (s_t - s_{t-1})/I_{t-1} \tag{4.2}$$

y_t is the profit rate of regulation capital. s_t is the profit of a certain industry in the current period and can be calculated by Eq. (4.1), s_{t-1} is the profit of the same industry in the last period, and I_{t-1} is the amount of investment of last period.

The second problem is profit rates fluctuate all the time. the number of profit rate at any time cannot be treated as a result of equilibrium, so we need to calculate the equilibrium profit rate. Tsoufidis and Tsaliki (2014) develop a method to calculate the equilibrium of certain industry using the time series data. This method is simply and powerful. Its main idea is to build an AR(1) process of profit rate:

$$r_t = a + br_{t-1} + u_t \tag{4.3}$$

Expand the equation above, we can get:

$$r_t = a\left(1 + b + b^2 + \cdots b^{n-1}\right) + b^n r_{t-n} + u_t + bu_{t-1} + \cdots + b^n u_{t-n}$$

Obviously, if r_t is stationary time series and $-1 < b < 1$, then $a\left(1 + b + b^2 + \cdots b^{n-1}\right)$ will converge to a/(1 – b), $b^n r_{t-n}$ will converge to 0, and the variance will converge to $\sigma^2/(1 - b)$. Therefore a/(1 – b) represents equilibrium profit rate.

The last problem is that we are not trying to estimate the equilibrium profit rate of a certain industry, but the average equilibrium profit rate of an industry among all countries and average equilibrium profit rate of a country with all its industries. Considering this, we cannot get our result only using time series data, we need to deal with the panel data. Fortunately, the more complex data structure doesn't bring much complexity in the method, we only need to estimate Eq. (4.3) in GMM method. Both System GMM and Differenced GMM is applicable.

Therefore, to estimate the equilibrium profit rate, we can get a profit rate of one industry in a certain country by Eq. (4.1), and substitute it into (4.2) to get the profit rate of regulation capital. Then it is easy to use this kind of profit rate to build Eq. (4.3), and apply GMM method to estimate this regression equation. To keep the result robust, we need to use Hampel Identifier method to drop the extreme value of profit rate from our data source (Wilcox 2003).

The data necessary to our approach can be obtained from WIOD database release 2013, which contains the input-output relationship, profit, labor hours input, and the stock of fixed capital of 35 industries in 27 EU economics and 13 important economies. This database covers about 85% of world total output, so using this database can investigate the major part of world economy.

Table 4.1 shows the result of estimation of 28 productive industries. We use the approach developed by Shaikh and Tonak (1997) to definite the productive industries, in which the productive economic activities should be regarded as the process of producing use value for the purpose of exchanging value. Under this definition, we treat: (1) Financial Intermediation, (2) Real Estate Activities, (3) Renting of M&Eq and Other Business Activities, (4) Public Admin and Defence; Compulsory Social Security, (5) Wholesale Trade and Commission Trade, (6) Retail Trade, (7) Sale, Maintenance and Repair of Motor Vehicles and Motorcycles; Retail Sale of Fuel as unproductive industries, and excludes them from our estimation.

The results are very interesting. Although there are some differences between the estimations of System GMM and Differenced GMM, the equilibrium profit rates calculated by the estimation are quite close between two methods. The similar equilibrium profit rates show the robustness of this approach.

We can find with the result that about two-thirds of industries' of profit rates are quite close to each other. Because the equilibrium profit rates of 17 industries under the estimation of differenced GMM and 18 industries under the estimation of System GMM are located in the narrow range of 0.13 ± 0.02. Although there are some industries' profit rates vary widely from this range, of course, the equalization of profit rate is not a result of the convergence of every industry. The industries whose profit rates are not close to the mean value can be divided into four categories: the first refers to the advantage of technology, like the high-technological manufacture. The second kind of industries are not tradable, like construction and education; the third category is not the industry following capitalist law of production, like agriculture, since a major part of its producers are individual producer not seek the maximized profit rate but maximized income. Only the fourth kind of industries is common but without profit rate equalization, like Textiles and Textile Products; Leather, Leather and Footwear; Pulp, Paper, Paper, Printing and Publishing; Wood and Products of Wood and Cork. However, these kinds of industries have a same character: locating in developing countries and are engaged in the unequal global value chain, so their lower profit rate may have some relationships with the monopoly power of multinational corporations, but for the purpose of this article, we are not tending to discuss this issue in detail. All we need to confirm is that most tradable industries in manufacturing and mining have equalized their profit rate, and the other industries are not able to reach this situation.

Table 4.2 shows the average profit rate of 40 countries. It is also very clear that there is no equilibrium profit rate for the average profit rate of countries, as there is no country group whose profit rates are close enough to each other.

Hence, we can confirm that there is a profit rate equalization process among industries worldwide and in the contrary, there is no profit rate equalization process among countries in the world market. We can make sure that international production price is transformed from the concept of international value and its foundation is the efficient international trade and the formation of the global market not the perfect mobility of capital across the border.

Table 4.1 The average profit rate by industry

	Differenced GMM			System GMM		
	a	b	a/(1 − b)	a	b	a/(1 − b)
Agriculture, hunting, forestry and fishing	0.02	−0.03	0.02	−0.01	0.02	0.02
Mining and quarrying	0.14***	−0.08*	0.13	−0.05	0.13***	0.12
Food, beverages and tobacco	0.12***	−0.06*	0.12	−0.03	0.12***	0.12
Textiles and textile products	0.06**	−0.26***	0.05	−0.11***	0.05**	0.05
Leather, leather and footwear	0.07**	−0.49***	0.04	−0.26***	0.05	0.04
Wood and products of wood and cork	0.07***	0.10*	0.08	0.09**	0.07***	0.08
Pulp, paper, paper, printing and publishing	0.09***	−0.09**	0.08	−0.04	0.08***	0.08
Coke, refined petroleum and nuclear fuel	0.18***	−0.56***	0.12	−0.31***	0.15**	0.11
Chemicals and chemical products	0.14***	−0.10***	0.12	−0.08***	0.13***	0.12
Rubber and plastics	0.14***	−0.23***	0.11	−0.08**	0.11***	0.10
Other non-metallic mineral	0.15***	−0.20***	0.13	−0.12***	0.14***	0.12
Basic metals and fabricated metal	0.15***	−0.18***	0.13	−0.06	0.13***	0.12
Machinery, Nec	0.17***	−0.10	0.16	−0.08	0.17***	0.16

(continued)

Table 4.1 (continued)

	Differenced GMM			System GMM		
	a	b	a/(1 − b)	a	b	a/(1 − b)
Electrical and optical equipment	0.12***	−0.02	0.12	0.01	0.12***	0.12
Transport equipment	0.17***	−0.45***	0.12	−0.31***	0.15***	0.12
Manufacturing, Nec; Recycling	0.17***	−0.31***	0.13	−0.12***	0.13***	0.12
Electricity, gas and water supply	0.10***	0.02	0.11	0.06*	0.10***	0.10
Construction	0.23***	−0.25***	0.18	−0.14***	0.20***	0.18
Repair of household goods	0.22***	−0.40***	0.16	−0.18***	0.17***	0.14
Hotels and restaurants	0.12***	0.01	0.12	0.01	0.12***	0.12
Inland transport	0.09***	−0.08*	0.08	−0.03	0.08***	0.08
Water transport	0.21***	−0.35***	0.15	−0.16***	0.16**	0.14
Air transport	0.08***	−0.08***	0.08	−0.08***	0.08***	0.08
Other supporting and auxiliary transport activities	0.14***	−0.11***	0.13	0.04	0.13***	0.13
Post and telecommunications	0.16***	−0.05	0.15	0.01	0.14***	0.15
Education	0.10***	−0.29***	0.08	−0.18***	0.09***	0.08
Health and social work	0.15***	−0.15***	0.13	−0.11***	0.15***	0.13
Other community, social and personal services	0.15***	−0.32***	0.12	−0.17***	0.13***	0.11

(*: p-value < 0.1, **: p-value < 0.05, ***: p-value < 0.01)

Table 4.2 The average profit rate by countries

	Differenced GMM			Systematic GMM		
	a	b	a/(1 − b)	a	b	a/(1 − b)
Australia	0.09***	−0.14***	0.08	0.08***	−0.07**	0.08
Austria	0.13***	−0.17***	0.11	0.12***	−0.07	0.11
Belgium	0.07***	−0.10**	0.06	0.06***	−0.07*	0.06
Bulgaria	0.29***	−0.25***	0.23	0.23***	−0.10***	0.21
Brazil	0.12***	−0.38***	0.09	0.12***	−0.26***	0.09
Canada	0.13***	−0.11**	0.12	0.11***	0.03	0.11
China	0.22***	0.14**	0.25	0.20***	0.20***	0.25
Cyprus	0.06**	−0.61***	0.03	0.07*	−0.34***	0.05
Czech	0.15***	−0.11**	0.13	0.14***	−0.04	0.14
Germany	0.16***	−0.33***	0.12	0.14***	−0.17***	0.12
Denmark	0.04***	−0.34***	0.03	0.04**	−0.21***	0.03
Spain	0.12***	−0.03	0.12	0.11***	0.04	0.12
Estonia	0.16***	−0.16***	0.13	0.14***	−0.09**	0.13
Finland	0.15***	−0.31***	0.12	0.14***	−0.16***	0.12
Frence	0.13***	−0.14***	0.11	0.12***	−0.03	0.11
UK	0.02	−0.01	0.02	0.02	−0.02	0.02
Greece	0.11**	−0.08***	0.10	0.11**	−0.08***	0.10
Hungary	0.17***	−0.20***	0.14	0.15***	−0.12***	0.14
Indonesia	0.31***	−0.43***	0.21	0.20**	−0.21***	0.17
India	0.13***	0.07	0.14	0.13***	0.05	0.14
Ireland	0.11***	−0.31***	0.08	0.09**	−0.18***	0.07
Italy	0.05**	−0.11***	0.05	0.05***	−0.07	0.05
Japan	0.00	−0.15***	0.00	0.00	−0.05	0.00
Korea	0.03	−0.07	0.03	0.03	−0.05	0.03
Lithuania	0.20***	−0.08	0.19	0.19***	−0.05	0.18
Luxemburg	0.07***	−0.21***	0.06	0.06***	−0.12***	0.05
Latvia	0.11***	−0.10*	0.10	0.11***	−0.09**	0.10
Mexico	0.10***	0.22***	0.13	0.12***	0.14***	0.14
Malta	0.11***	−0.37***	0.08	0.10***	−0.25***	0.08
Netherland	0.14***	−0.36***	0.11	0.12***	0.18***	0.15
Poland	0.25***	−0.12***	0.22	0.24***	−0.07***	0.22
Portugal	0.06***	−0.16***	0.05	0.05**	−0.04	0.04
Romania	0.22***	−0.25***	0.17	0.19***	−0.16***	0.16
Russia	0.33***	−0.43***	0.23	0.26***	−0.21***	0.21

(continued)

Table 4.2 (continued)

Slovakia	0.20***	−0.25***	0.16	0.18***	−0.17***	0.16
Slovenia	0.24***	−0.45***	0.16	0.15**	−0.18***	0.13
Sweden	0.12***	−0.09	0.11	0.11***	−0.05	0.11
Turkey	0.15***	−0.03	0.15	0.14***	0.03	0.14
Taiwan	0.03**	−0.18***	0.03	0.03**	−0.12***	0.03
US	0.07***	−0.03	0.07	0.07***	−0.04	0.07

(*: p-value < 0.1, **: p-value < 0.05, ***: p-value < 0.01)

4.3 Reconstructing and Measuring Unequal Exchange

4.3.1 Rethinking Unequal Exchange and Its Critiques

As we introduce the category of international value, we should review the criticisms again. First, we find that unequal exchange theory could survive under critique 1. Both Emmanuel and Critics use the equalization of regional profit rate as the foundation of international production price, but in fact, the international production price is transformed from international value, and international value is an industrial category, not a regional one. As productivity vary from country to country, national values in countries are different too, so are the profit rates. And after international value transformed into international production price, nothing would change.

Critique 3 is also a case that critics are wrong. Emmanuel's theory doesn't specify which kind of value is transferred, because in the case of complete division of labor, as one commodity just has one producer, the international value is equivalent to national value. But in every critic's formal model, although there are incomplete division of labor conditions, they only measure national value's transfer. As Shaikh (1979, 1980) has pointed out, one may suffer from an outflow of national value while enjoying the inflow of international value, vice versa. But if we focus on the transfer of international value, there is no doubt that higher capital organic composition or lower surplus value rate would lead to an inflow of value.

However, the second criticism hits the point, and exposes the fatal flaw of Emmanuel's theory. Lower wage does not mean higher surplus value rate, so there is no certain relationship between developing countries' low wage and value's outflow. Moreover, the base of international production price is international value, and its deviation from the base is determined by the average composition of capital organic and average exploitation rate of a certain industry worldwide. Therefore, even one country's exploitation rate is high, as if other countries' exploitation rate in the same industry is low, the average exploitation of this industry in the global level would not high enough, and this country could avoid unequal exchange's bad effect.

But this criticism is only fatal to Emmanuel's theory, not to unequal exchange itself (or the second kind of unequal exchange exactly). This kind of unequal exchange is based on the deviation between international production price and international value. If developing countries or peripheries are mostly engaged in the industries that the former is lower than the latter, then unequal exchange exists, the lower wage of a certain country is not the only possible access to get such a result.

As mentioned above, organic composition and exploitation rate are two main factors related to the deviation between production price and value. The organic composition is mainly an industrial factor. If industries of high organic compositions are more likely to locate at core countries and low organic composition industries tend to locate at peripheral countries, then an unequal exchange would happen. Such an industrial distribution is quite probable, as the high organic composition is associated with high productivity and advanced technology, and most core countries are capital-abundant. Bauer (2000) and Grossman (1992) had demonstrated this approach in about 100 years ago.

The rate of surplus value is a regional factor, so one country's surplus value may not be directly related to the international value composition of a certain industry. However, if peripheral countries have similar industrial structure and similar higher surplus value rate, as a result, the industries that peripheries most engaged in would have a higher surplus value in the extent of international value, and hence unequal exchange occurs.

Now we can see that following the logic above, we get a totally new version of unequal exchange based on the international value transformation, this version of unequal exchange doesn't rely on the domestic income distribution like Emmanuel's, but based on the bias of international division of labor, international division of labor could be explained by the global capital accumulation. Hence, this theory has a closer relationship with the orthodox Marxist economics.

It is worth mentioning, although the three categories of unequal exchange have the same content, value transfer, they are of different causations and different results. The unequal exchange we care about in this paper is caused by international division of labor and this kind of value transfer results in the transfer of use value or wealth. Because there is only one international value for a certain kind of use value, as the price deviates from the international value, the producer whose products have higher price claim a larger part of use value and vice versa. So this kind of unequal exchange has a very straight relationship with uneven development. And the unequal exchange caused by the market price deviation from international production price is caused by market power of monopoly power of the multinational corporation of core capitalist countries, and as the international production price also have an one-to-one correspondence with the used value, so its impact on uneven development between cores and peripheries are also clearly. However, the first kind of unequal exchange, which is caused by the gap between national value and international value, is a consequence of productivity difference or the level of development itself, and one kind of use value may have many national values. Therefore, the producer of higher national value suffers from value transfer, but it is not clear whether this value transfer is also a kind of use value transfer. As we focus on the unequal exchange based on international value transformation, this confusing problem of the first kind of unequal exchange is not discussed further.

4.3.2 The Measurement of Unequal Exchange

The discussion above just proves that unequal exchange is probable. The only way to confirm its existence is to introduce some method to calculate the international value transfer between countries, there have been some empirical studies on this topic. But all of them just calculate the value transfer without specifying which kind of value is transferred, in fact, they all used national input-output table and calculate every industry's national value (i.e. total labor input), and compare the labor import and labor export in the international trade. It is obvious that transferred value calculated in this approach is a combination of unequal exchange caused by productivity gap, international value transformation and marketing power, while our theory only cares about the value transfer due to international value transformation. So we need a new method to fulfill our target.

Our method is inspired by Marelli's research in 1983. His study is to measure the value transfer between regions inside Italy. The core idea is to treat Italy economy as a whole, and measure value and production price of every industry, then divide them in a certain industry to each region by this region's proportion of the gross output of this industry. There is a difference between the value and production price in every industry of one region, and sum up all these differences in one region, the sum is the total transferred value caused by value transformation. And it is easy to apply this approach to the international unequal exchange, we can just substitute the regions by countries. So the calculation is divided into three steps: (a) Treating the world economy as an entirety and calculating the international value and international production price of every industry in this economy (b) Dividing these variables to every country, and then sum up them in the country level, to get the total international value and production price produced in every country. (c) Use the total international production price to minus total international value of every country and then get the total transferred value caused by the unequal exchange.

The second and third steps are very easy to realize if the first step is done, so the most important task is to measure the international value and international production price. Based on the pioneering work by Morishima (1973) and Ochoa (1989), there are modern methods of value measurement introduced by the literature. However, given that these methods mainly focus on value measurement within the boundaries of a country on the basis of the input-output table of the country, they are not capable of measuring the international value of commodities worldwide. In addition, as far as the national value within the boundaries of the country is concerned, there are also some deviations, as they fail to take into account the value differences between imported intermediate products and intermediate products produced in the country. In that account, based on Output Database (WIOD) (Dietzenbacher et al. 2013), we have extended the value measurement to the international level.

Obviously, it is a very complicated task, as international value cannot be invisible even in the world input-output table. But, fortunately, we can start at the national value.

Considering there is a world input-output table, and assuming that there are N countries and n sectors, we can express the labor input-output structure by the formula below:

$$\left[\begin{pmatrix} A^{11} & \cdots & A^{1N} \\ \vdots & \ddots & \vdots \\ A^{N1} & \cdots & A^{NN} \end{pmatrix} + \begin{pmatrix} D^{11} & \cdots & D^{1N} \\ \vdots & \ddots & \vdots \\ D^{N1} & \cdots & D^{NN} \end{pmatrix}\right]\begin{pmatrix} \lambda^{1} \\ \cdots \\ \lambda^{N} \end{pmatrix} + \begin{pmatrix} l^{1} \\ \cdots \\ l^{N} \end{pmatrix} = \begin{pmatrix} \lambda^{1} \\ \cdots \\ \lambda^{N} \end{pmatrix} \tag{4.4}$$

where $\boldsymbol{A}^{xy}$ is an intermediate input square matrix that consists of a_{ij}^{xy} and reflects the consumption of the inputs of country y by the production processes of country x (in which, a_{ij}^{xy} represents the demand of each unit of product of the *i*th sector of country x for the intermediate inputs of the *j*th sector of country y). $\boldsymbol{D}^{xy}$ is a fixed capital depreciation square matrix that consists of d_{ij}^{xy} and reflects the depreciation of the fixed capitals produced by country y and needed by country x during the production processes (in which, d_{ij}^{xy} represents the depreciation of the fixed capitals produced by the *j*th sector of country y and needed by each unit of product in the production processes of the *i*th sector of country x). $\boldsymbol{\lambda}^{x}$ is the national value column vector of the *i*th country that consists of λ_{i}^{x} (in which, λ_{i}^{x} represents the domestic value of each unit of product of the *i*th sector of country x); $\boldsymbol{l}^{x}$ is the domestic value column vector of the *i*th country that consists of l_{i}^{x} (in which, l_{i}^{x} represents the direct labor input of each unit of product of the *i*th sector of country x).

We can also express them by a more condensed formula:

$$(\boldsymbol{A}^{C} + \boldsymbol{D}^{C})\boldsymbol{\lambda}^{C} + \boldsymbol{l}^{C} = \boldsymbol{\lambda}^{C} \tag{4.5}$$

We use the superscript C to represent various matrices used in the accounting of the national value. That is $\mathbf{A}^{C} = \begin{pmatrix} A^{11} & \cdots & A^{1N} \\ \vdots & \ddots & \vdots \\ A^{N1} & \cdots & A^{NN} \end{pmatrix}$, $\mathbf{D}^{C} = \begin{pmatrix} D^{11} & \cdots & D^{1N} \\ \vdots & \ddots & \vdots \\ D^{N1} & \cdots & D^{NN} \end{pmatrix}$, $\mathbf{l}^{C} = \begin{pmatrix} l^{1} \\ \cdots \\ l^{N} \end{pmatrix}$, $\lambda^{C} = \begin{pmatrix} \lambda^{1} \\ \cdots \\ \lambda^{N} \end{pmatrix}$.

Based on the above formula, we can obtain the expression of the national value:

$$\boldsymbol{\lambda}^{C} = (\mathbf{I} - \mathbf{A}^{C} - \mathbf{D}^{C})^{-1}\mathbf{l}^{C}$$

In the above algorithms **A**, **D** and so forth are all required to be physical matrices, however, in reality, input-output table data are all value-type data. Fortunately, as demonstrated by Marelli (1983), value-type input-output tables can fully satisfy our requirements, and what we need to do is to adjust the estimation method in the following manner:

$$\boldsymbol{\lambda}^{C*} = (\boldsymbol{I} - \boldsymbol{A}^{C*} - \boldsymbol{D}^{C*})^{-1}\boldsymbol{l}^{C*} \tag{4.6}$$

where for each matrix, the elements therein can be expressed as $a_{ij}^{xy*} = a_{ij}^{xy} m_j^y \big/ a_{ij}^{xy*} = a_{ij}^{xy} m_j^y m_i^x m_i^x$, $d_{ij}^{xy*} = d_{ij}^{xy} m_j^y \big/ d_{ij}^{xy} m_j^y m_i^x m_i^x$, $l_i^{x*} = l_i^x / l_i^x m_i^x m_i^x$ and $\lambda_i^{x*} = \lambda_i^x / \lambda_i^x m_i^x m_i^x$. m_i^x represent the total output of i industry in country x measured by the market price, that is $m_i^x = q_i^x \tau_i^x$, in which q_i^x is the quantity of output of i industry in country x, and τ_i^x is the market price of the same industry.

The above formula indicates that, even though we only have intermediate inputs and total capital depreciation of $a_{ij}^{xy} m_j^y$ and $d_{ij}^{xy} m_j^y$ in the value-type input-output table bearing market prices, we can still obtain the value $\lambda_i^{x*} = \lambda_i^x / m_i^x$ contained by each unit of currency in an industry through dividing the elements in $\boldsymbol{A}, \boldsymbol{D}, \boldsymbol{l}$ and $\boldsymbol{\lambda}$ by the total output of the industry. And if we need the total value of the national value of one industry in a country, we can get it by the formula: $\lambda_i^x = \lambda_i^{x*} m_i^x$.

In fact, we do not care about national value, but based on the national value, in the following section, we proceed to calculate the international value. The international value is supposed to be determined by the necessary labor time of producing the product worldwide, which is further determined by the mean technical level and mean labor intensity level of the world on the whole. We use the superscript I to represent various coefficients and results under international mean technical and labor conditions, based on which the international value can be expressed by the following formulas:

$$\begin{aligned} a_{11}^I \lambda_1^I + a_{12}^I \lambda_2^I + \cdots + a_{1n}^I \lambda_n^I + l_1^I &= \lambda_1^I \\ a_{21}^I \lambda_1^I + a_{22}^I \lambda_2^I + \cdots + a_{2n}^I \lambda_n^I + l_2^I &= \lambda_2^I \\ &\cdots \\ a_{n1}^I \lambda_1^I + a_{n2}^I \lambda_2^I + \cdots + a_{nn}^I \lambda_n^I + l_n^I &= \lambda_n^I \end{aligned}$$

or

$$\boldsymbol{\lambda}^{\boldsymbol{I}} = (\mathbf{I} - \mathbf{A}^{\boldsymbol{I}} + \mathbf{D}^{\boldsymbol{I}})^{-1}\mathbf{l}^{\boldsymbol{I}} \tag{4.7}$$

Then, how we determine the coefficients under international mean technical and labor conditions? Apparently, we have no way to determine various coefficients, but we can still solve the problem by starting with the value-type input-output table. By assuming:

$$a_{ij}^I m_i^I = \sum_x \sum_y a_{ij}^{xy} m_i^y,\ d_{ij}^I m_i^I = \sum_x \sum_y d_{ij}^{xy} m_i^y, l_i^I = \sum_x l_i^x$$

Similar to m_i^x, m_i^I is the total output of i industry worldwide measured by the market price.

We can obtain

$$a_{ij}^{I*} = a_{ij}^{I} m_j^I / m_i^I,\ d_{ij}^{I*} = d_{ij}^{I} m_j^I / m_i^I,\ l_i^{I*} = l_i^I / m_i^I,\ \lambda_i^{I*} = \lambda_i^I / m_i^I$$

And the expression for the international value

$$\boldsymbol{\lambda}^{I*} = (\boldsymbol{I} - \mathbf{A}^{I*} - \mathbf{D}^{I*})^{-1}\mathbf{l}^{I^*} \tag{4.8}$$

That is, with regard to the intermediate input coefficient and fixed capital depreciation coefficient, we first add up all the outputs produced by the industry j in various countries and consumed by the industry i in each country, and then further add up the consumptions by all the countries. Finally, we divide the sum by the total output of the industry worldwide. With regard to the labor input coefficient, we directly add up the labor input hours worldwide and divide the sum by the total worldwide output.

The reason for adopting this method to obtain the international value is that it has the same origin as both the compilation logic of input-output tables and the logic of value accounting within the boundaries of a country. The input-output table within a country is obtained exactly by adding up the intermediate inputs, capital depreciation and labor input of various enterprises in various regions under various technologies, and is deemed as an approximate expression of the production technologies of an industry of a country. By the same token, to obtain the input-output table reflecting production technologies worldwide, the most direct way is to further add up the above elements worldwide and to take the table prepared as an expression of the mean production technologies of the world.

On international production price, the method is very similar. The expression is below:

$$(\boldsymbol{A}^I + \boldsymbol{K}^I + \boldsymbol{W}^I)\boldsymbol{p}(1 + r) = \boldsymbol{p} \tag{4.9}$$

The meanings of $\boldsymbol{A}^I$ is same with the situation of international value, $\boldsymbol{K}^I$ is a fixed capital stock squared matrix, in which k_{ij}^I represents the capital stock produced by j industry and used in I industry to produce one unit of products. $\boldsymbol{W}^I$ is the real wage matrix, in which w_{ij}^I represents the amount of j industry's commodity consumed by workers in i industry to produce one unit of products and $\boldsymbol{p}$ is the international production price vector, and p_i represents the international production price of i industry. r represents the equilibrium profit rate of every industry.

It is worth mentioning that in the calculation of production price, as shown above, we use the fixed capital stock matrix $\boldsymbol{K}^I$ instead of fixed capital depreciation matrix $\boldsymbol{D}^I$ because the production price is related to a process of profit equalization according to the volume of advanced capital. So the formation of production price should be based on the stock of fixed capital not the depreciation, in other words, the flow of fixed capital.

We can transform the formula above to:

$$(\boldsymbol{A}^I + \boldsymbol{K}^I + \boldsymbol{W}^I)\boldsymbol{p} = \frac{1}{1 + r}\boldsymbol{p} \tag{4.10}$$

And now it is clear that $\boldsymbol{p}$ is the eigenvector and $\frac{1}{1+r}$ is the eigenvalue of the matrix $\boldsymbol{A}^I + \boldsymbol{K}^I + \boldsymbol{W}^I$. According to Perron-Frobenius Theorem, if $\boldsymbol{A}^I + \boldsymbol{K}^I + \boldsymbol{W}^I$ is nonnegative and indecomposable, then the biggest eigenvalue corresponds to the only positive eigenvector, that is, under the minimum positive profit rate r; there is the unique meaningful solution of production price $\boldsymbol{p}$. Of course, this method also needs the physical matrixes of $\boldsymbol{A}^I$, $\boldsymbol{K}^I$ and $\boldsymbol{W}^I$. But we can also use Marelli's approach mentioned above to get the right result using value form of input-output data.

In this way, we constructed an accounting system from national value to international production price. However, there are still some details that need further processing.

First, WIOD only contains 40 countries and regions. Although it contains almost all the major economies in the world, apparently all of them consume intermediate inputs of other countries besides their own. However, in WIOD, these intermediate inputs are uniformly added up as those provided by other countries to us. When calculating the international value, this does not create particular complicacy, as we already include these intermediate inputs, which means that the total intermediate input of the 40 countries and regions obtained does not produce any deviation. The problem lies with the calculation of the national value because these intermediate inputs come from different countries and thus have different national values. But we do not have a satisfactory method of solving this problem, and the only feasible assumption is that the national values of these intermediate inputs are consistent with the national value of the country using it so that we can add them up in $\boldsymbol{A}^{xx}$. Fortunately, in most cases, the intermediate inputs of other countries only account for an extremely small part and do not impose any substantial influence on the estimation.

Second, WIOD only provides related data on intermediate inputs in various industries, and, for depreciation of fixed capitals, it only provides the total amount of fixed capitals consumed by an industry without offering any information about their source industries. Thus, we need to break down the total amount. With regard to $\boldsymbol{D}^C$, by assuming that the fixed capitals consumed by each industry and its depreciation structure are consistent with its investment structure, we can obtain what we need in the following manner:

$$d_{ij}^{xy} m_i^x = d_i^x m_i^x \eta_j^{xy} \tag{4.11}$$

where d_i^x is the overall fixed capital depreciation coefficient of sector i of country x, that is, the total fixed capital depreciation/total output. k_i^x is the overall fixed capital stock coefficient of sector i of country x, that is, the fixed capital stock/total output; η_j^{xy} is the proportion of the output of industry j of country y used by country x in its investment in the total investment.

Similarly, with regard to $\boldsymbol{D}^I$, we have

$$d_{ij}^I m_i^I = d_i^I m_i^I \eta_j^I \tag{4.12}$$

Third, according to the logic of Marxist economics, not all sectors of an economy can create value. Here we adopt the method proposed by Shaikh and Tonak (1997), where productive sectors are sectors engaged in the production of certain use value for the purpose of exchange. By this definition, the differentiation between material production and non-material production becomes unimportant, and, as long as the private labor is socialized by means of exchange, we take it as productive labor. In that way, based on the above definition, some sectors, like circulation sectors, financial sectors, and government sectors, do not create any form of use value. Thus, under the classification of WIOD, we deem the financial intermediation industry, Renting of m&eq and other business activities industry, real estate activities industry, retail trade industry, wholesale trade industry and public admin & defense sector as non-productive sectors, and exclude them from the accounting. At the same time, although the private households with employed person industry should have been counted as a productive sector, considering the lack of data for most countries, we have excluded it from the accounting for data integrity.

Fourth, the result we get about values are of the form of labor times, and the production price is relative price without dimension. If we want to calculate the transferred value, we need to compare them two. So, we need to normalize them to the common dimension, dollar. Following Ochoa's (1989), we have:

$$\mu = \sum_i m_i / \sum_i \lambda_i, \nu = \sum_i m_i / \sum_i p_i$$
$$\lambda_i' = \mu\lambda_i, p_i' = \nu\lambda_i$$

That is to say, we can normalize the value and production price by the ratio of them to market price.

Finally, according to the tradition of Marxist economics, equal amounts of unskilled and skilled labor embody different values in commodities. The traditional practice (Ochoa 1989) is to assume that wage disparities reflect conversion relations between unskilled and skilled labor, based on which mutual ratios of wages per unit of labor time in different sectors are employed to convert their labor input coefficients. Theoretically, as noted by Foot and Webber (1983) and Webber (1987), this calculation method causes the value to depend on wages (that is, prices), while essentially the former should have been employed for the interpretation of the latter. It is logically contradictory, and the fluctuations of wages will result in instability in calculations and incomparability of labor at different time points.

In the view of infeasibility of adopting wage or other similar methods using a price structure, we have decided to follow Webber (1987), and to treat the labor in different sectors as qualitatively identical labor based on the following considerations. First, the reductions of unskilled and skilled labor are derived from discussions under an abstract and pure environment of commodity exchange. However, under the system of capitalist employment, this reduced objective environment no longer exists. So, theoretically, reductions of this type cannot be reflected in reality by any variable, and, correspondingly, their role becomes unimportant. Second, the capitalist labor process is a process of continuous de-skilling that increasingly manifests labor as unskilled labor, so the differentiation between unskilled and skilled labor for the accounting of the value in the capitalist production process is no longer as significant as in a small commodity production society or early stage of capitalism (Braverman 1974). Finally, and most importantly, the classification of industries currently in use has in fact gone through a considerable degree of aggregation, and each sector contains labor of different degrees of complexity, therefore, there is no reason to think that, among these major industry categories, some have a higher proportion of complex labor or higher degree of labor complexity than others. (However, Webber (1987) has proved that, although the degrees of labor complexity may differ within an industry, the aggregation method currently in use can still correctly reflect the value created by the sector.)

4.3.3 Estimation Results

After that, we calculate the ratio of transferred value to the gross output of every country in the world IO table from 1995 to 2009. And the result is shown in Table 4.3. We divided the countries into three groups: Countries suffering from the unequal exchange, benefiting from it and changing their roles from value outflow countries to value inflow countries.

First, we confirm that unequal exchange does exist, developing countries in Asian, Latin American and Eastern and South Europe experiencing value outflow and developed countries in North America, Western and Northern Europe enjoying value inflow. And this agrees with the conjecture of unequal exchange theory.

Second, we find that unequal exchange has a significant effect on these countries' economy, as the ratio are considerable in any sense. Most developed countries enjoy transferred value from 5 to 10% of total output, and value outflow from developing countries can be up to 20% of total output average, and in some cases this ratio can reach 50%. Value transfer of such scale would surely have great impact on development on a certain country. As we mentioned above, such value transfer means the transfer of wealth between countries that influences the level of development directly. And such value transfer would also have further impact on the capital accumulation because the quantity of surplus value and the profit rate have been changed among countries by unequal exchange.

Third, there is a very interesting result that we are not expected in our theory, although the proportion of value inflow to output in developed countries remains constant, the ratio of value outflow to output is decreasing in some developing countries in the period of the sample. In the traditional viewpoint of unequal exchange, the unequal exchange is a stationary mechanism, but here there is a trend for many developing countries to escape from it.

There may be four explanations for such a phenomenon:

(1) The value transfer is becoming relatively small because of the rapid growth of developing countries. As some developing countries like China and India

Table 4.3 Value transfer as a proportion of total output in 40 countries from 1995 to 2009 (%)

	1995	1996	1997	1998	1999	2000	2001	2002	2003	2004	2005	2006	2007	2008	2009
Countries suffering from unequal exchange															
Bulgaria	−51.6	−66.6	−75.9	−57.3	−50.5	−42.9	−38.3	−31.1	−45.4	−26.4	−25.0	−21.6	−14.0	−17.5	−7.6
China	−40.1	−47.3	−37.3	−36.5	−32.4	−34.6	−32.4	−29.8	−30.3	−22.6	−20.5	−20.1	−17.4	−16.8	−15.2
Cyprus	−24.0	−24.0	−20.0	−21.3	−20.1	−17.5	−18.3	−18.4	−17.6	−14.9	−15.0	−11.4	−7.8	−4.3	−2.9
Spain	−10.2	−10.4	−9.7	−9.8	−7.8	−8.9	−9.5	−9.9	−6.0	−9.3	−8.4	−6.9	−5.3	−3.3	−2.7
Brazil	−11.5	−14.8	−9.7	−9.7	−11.1	−10.3	−10.6	−12.0	−25.6	−15.5	−13.8	−12.0	−11.1	−11.1	−8.7
Turkey	−37.6	−48.8	−32.6	−41.6	−29.7	−34.2	−27.0	−31.6	−42.9	−32.6	−35.2	−32.7	−27.5	−24.0	−21.5
Mexico	−6.0	−14.0	−7.2	−6.7	−5.3	−7.2	−7.4	−6.2	−10.0	−5.7	−6.3	−5.1	−3.9	−3.1	−5.1
Estonia	−21.2	−20.5	−13.9	−14.2	−3.8	−5.9	−6.4	−5.4	−5.3	−3.9	−5.0	−4.2	−4.5	−1.4	4.1
Greece	−34.3	−37.4	−30.3	−29.6	−28.4	−27.2	−25.6	−22.2	−22.7	−16.1	−14.8	−11.0	−6.2	−4.0	−3.4
Hungary	−26.7	−34.6	−18.6	−15.9	−13.2	−13.7	−15.7	−12.5	−12.3	−6.6	−4.6	−3.8	−2.1	−1.7	0.9
Ireland	−19.0	−14.6	−9.2	−5.4	−4.6	−1.6	−4.2	−1.7	1.9	−3.7	−1.4	−0.7	1.2	4.9	9.7
Lithuania	−42.8	−56.1	−34.1	−28.9	−26.1	−21.6	−18.8	−13.4	−17.1	−11.0	−13.7	−13.4	−15.4	−9.4	−3.6
Poland	−24.1	−31.1	−20.4	−20.4	−15.0	−18.0	−17.4	−11.6	−14.9	−11.7	−12.2	−12.1	−12.5	−9.8	−6.0
Portugal	−13.2	−12.9	−10.4	−10.1	−7.1	−9.4	−9.1	−8.0	−5.5	−6.3	−4.5	−3.4	0.4	0.7	2.6
Russia	−0.4	−12.9	0.0	−0.7	−12.1	−10.7	−10.7	−3.3	−10.2	3.2	5.2	5.1	5.3	4.3	6.9
Romania	−51.9	−64.6	−50.3	−48.5	−38.7	−40.7	−49.5	−36.7	−55.7	−43.4	−33.8	−32.0	−23.9	−24.7	−20.3
India	−43.9	−45.0	−40.0	−48.5	−59.2	−52.1	−50.2	−51.0	−59.4	−44.9	−41.5	−41.6	−41.2	−40.9	−40.6
Indonesia	−51.7	−65.8	−50.6	−53.7	−55.4	−56.0	−55.2	−48.2	−63.5	−44.3	−47.2	−45.5	−41.1	−37.2	−33.3
Latvia	−27.7	−26.1	−16.1	−14.2	−9.7	−11.6	−15.4	−14.7	−16.8	−17.8	−19.9	−17.9	−18.4	−12.7	−7.4
Countries experiencing the role switching in unequal exchange															
Korea	−7.6	−3.8	−4.1	−3.1	−1.5	−0.1	1.1	2.1	4.8	3.9	4.7	5.1	6.0	7.2	5.3
Demark	−6.2	−3.0	−2.6	−1.2	−0.6	1.2	1.2	2.5	4.3	4.6	6.2	6.8	7.6	9.1	10.5

(continued)

Table 4.3 (continued)

Slovakia	−2.1	−5.7	−0.6	−1.8	3.3	2.4	1.9	5.5	4.7	7.6	4.4	4.6	5.0	5.8	7.4
Slovenia	−3.5	−3.1	−4.1	−2.7	0.3	−2.5	−1.2	−0.8	4.2	0.8	0.5	1.3	0.9	2.0	4.1
Netherland	−2.8	−2.7	−1.5	−0.6	−1.3	−0.2	0.9	2.4	2.0	3.8	3.7	3.5	3.6	5.1	5.5
Taiwan	−3.0	−0.6	2.3	4.2	6.2	6.4	7.1	9.1	9.8	9.8	9.7	9.8	9.8	8.6	7.9
Countries benefiting from unequal exchange															
Australia	6.1	5.8	5.9	5.2	4.4	1.8	−0.6	3.5	2.4	2.6	3.6	5.3	5.6	4.4	7.6
Austria	4.7	8.1	5.5	6.2	6.9	6.3	7.4	7.8	11.2	9.0	9.9	10.6	9.6	10.3	11.9
Belgium	7.4	9.9	8.5	9.0	10.4	9.2	9.0	9.8	11.8	9.9	11.4	10.9	10.6	11.0	11.2
Canada	4.9	4.0	4.3	3.4	2.3	4.1	3.8	2.8	3.8	3.3	3.8	4.3	4.7	4.6	6.0
Czech	2.9	0.7	2.3	2.2	4.1	0.8	1.3	3.3	5.3	4.8	3.1	4.5	4.6	5.4	7.1
Germany	9.8	13.7	9.8	10.8	10.0	10.2	10.6	12.2	15.5	13.3	13.7	13.3	12.7	12.8	14.8
Finland	2.5	8.2	4.3	5.6	4.8	5.0	5.8	6.7	12.7	8.3	6.9	8.0	5.6	6.9	8.3
France	7.0	5.6	7.4	6.9	−3.5	−1.6	−1.3	−0.5	0.2	0.5	0.7	1.5	1.3	2.2	3.0
UK	13.6	15.8	15.6	17.0	16.5	18.3	18.0	17.2	20.0	16.2	19.0	20.0	19.5	19.4	19.6
Italy	2.2	4.2	3.7	3.4	6.8	3.4	3.6	3.7	4.5	2.7	3.3	4.3	4.0	4.5	4.6
Japan	6.5	10.8	7.3	6.7	6.3	6.3	6.4	6.5	9.0	6.7	6.5	6.9	6.9	7.2	6.7
Luxemburg	14.9	19.5	16.8	16.1	19.6	17.3	17.4	15.0	21.7	16.4	16.8	19.9	20.6	21.0	22.6
Malta	6.8	6.2	7.1	7.3	7.5	9.4	8.6	7.7	6.8	10.2	9.6	11.4	10.5	13.3	15.1
Sweden	14.0	18.3	16.0	15.9	14.2	16.0	16.7	17.2	21.2	17.8	18.7	17.9	16.8	17.3	17.8
US	7.2	9.5	7.6	7.1	7.5	9.0	9.4	8.1	9.4	6.7	6.9	7.8	8.1	9.2	9.2

experienced fast growth and the total output of these economies are becoming larger and larger, if the extent of unequal exchange does not growing as fast as the total output, the ratios of value outflow decrease. To those developed countries, as they did not enjoy fast growth, the ratios remain constant. Obviously, this is a very straight and clear explanation of such a phenomenon, but there are still some other factors worth mentioning.

(2) The sample does not cover enough developing countries. As there are only a few developing countries is contained in the World IO database, so it is hard to say our samples are representative enough. In fact, if we focus on the developing countries in the traditional sense in our samples (that is to exclude the Former Soviet-Eastern Europe states), only China experiences a declining trend of value outflow.

(3) This could be due to the upgrading industrial structure in developing countries (Nakajima and Izumi 1995). And such a process may be a consequence of the decreasing proportion of value outflow industries in developing countries, that is there is a convergent tendency between core and peripheries in industrial structure. Otherwise, this can be a result of decreasing proportion of productive industries in developed countries, that is, the de-industrialization process makes the core countries shift their productive industries to the peripheries. This means although developing countries experience a declining of unequal exchange in trade, but the formation of unequal exchange is changed, and core countries may focus on the unproductive industries to claim more value produced in peripheries.

(4) This may be also a result of the convergence of the gap of the organic composition of capital and rate of surplus value among industries. Although the international division of labor remains stable, the convergence of this two variables can make the value transfer among industries decline, and as the value transfer among countries, as mentioned above, results from industrial value transfer, so that the value transfer and unequal exchange among cores and peripheries decreases. It is quite possible as the accumulation of capital may both raise organic composition of capital and depress the exploitation rate. Because capitalists pursue super surplus value by developing the productivity which has a very close relationship with organic composition, and the excessive accumulation may exhaust the industrial reserve army and raise the wage in short term.

If the second and third explanation is right, the result may have a very interesting impact on unequal exchange, but this need a research in detail, which is not available in this paper, we hope it can be finished in the future.

4.4 Conclusion

In this paper, we review Emmanuel's unequal exchange theory by introducing the concept of international value. Considering international value, there is no relationship between the formation of international production price and the perfect mobility of capital among countries. An empirical estimation of equalization of profit rate based on the framework of regulation capital is used to certify this viewpoint. By doing this, we find that the most fatal critique to this theory is not correct in fact. However, this concept also implies that there is no direct relation between real wage and value transfer, so unequal exchange should also be reconstructed under the framework of the international division of labor. We also examine the existence of unequal exchange by calculating the gap between international production price and international value, i.e. the volume of transferred value of 40 countries, and finds that unequal exchange does exist and is significant enough to affect the development of one country. And there is a very interesting phenomenon in the result of empirical studying. There are several developing countries escaping from the unequal exchange very fast, and we offer several probable reasons, but further research is required to confirm which one is right or most important.

References

Bauer O (2000) The question of nationalities and social democracy. University of Minnesota Press, Minneapolis. Originally published in 1907 as Die Nationalitätenfrage und die Sozialdemokratie. Verlag der Wiener Volksbuchhandlung, Vienna

Birkan A (2015) A brief overview of the theory of unequal exchange and its critiques. Int J Humanit Soc Sci 5(4):155–162

Braverman H (1974) Labor and monopoly capital: the degradation of work in the twentieth century. Monthly Review Press, New York

Chandra N (1986) Theories of unequal exchange: a critique Emmanuel and Amin. Econ Polit Wkly 21(30):PE77–PE84

Cockshott P, Cottrell A (1998) Does Marx need to transform. In: Bellofiore R (ed) Marxian economics: a reappraisal, vol 2. Springer, New York

De Janvry A, Kramer F (1979) The limits of unequal exchange. Rev Radic Polit Econ 11(3):3–15

Dietzenbacher E, Los B, Stehrer R et al (2013) The construction of world input–output tables in the WIOD project. Econ Syst Res 25(1):71–98

Emmanuel A (1972) Unequal exchange: a study of the imperialism of trade. Monthly Review Press, New York

Foot S, Webber M (1983) Unequal exchange and uneven development. Environ Plan D 1:281–304

Foot S, Webber M (1984) The measurement of unequal exchange. Environ Plan A 16(7):927–947

Gibson B (1980) Unequal exchange: theoretical issues and empirical findings. Rev Radic Polit Econ 12(3):15–35

Grossmann H (1992) The law of accumulation and breakdown of the capitalist system. Pluto Press, London. Originally published as Das Akkumulations- und Zusammenbruchsgesetz des kapitalistischen Systems, Hirschfeld: Zugleich eine Krisentheorie, 1929

Howard C, King J (2014) A history of marxian economics, vol II: 1929–1990. Princeton University Press, Princeton

Houston D, Paus E (1987) The theory of unequal exchange: an indictment. Rev Radic Polit Econ 19(1):90–97

Liossatos P (1980) Unequal exchange and regional disparities. Pap Reg Sci Assoc 45(1):87–103

Mandel E (1975) Late capitalism. Humanities Press, London

Marelli E (1983) Empirical estimation of intersectoral and interregional transfers of surplus value: the case of Italy. J Reg Sci 23(1):49–70

Morishima M (1973) Marx's economics: a dual theory of value and growth. Cambridge University Press, Cambridge
Nakajima A, Izumi H (1995) Economic development and unequal exchange among nations: analysis of U.S., Japan, and South Korea. Rev Radic Polit Econ 27(3): 86–94
Ochoa E (1989) Values, prices, and wage-profit curves in the US economy. Cambridge J Econ 13:413–429
Shaikh A (1979) Foreign trade and the law of value: part I. Sci Soc 42(3):281–302
Shaikh A (1980) Foreign trade and the law of value: part II. Sci Soc 44(1):27–57
Shaikh A (2008) Competition and industrial rates of return. In: Arestis P, Eatwell J (eds) Issues in Economic Development and Globalisation. Festschrift in Honor of Ajit Singh, Palgrave MacMillan, London
Shaikh A, Tonak E (1997) Measuring the wealth of nations. Cambridge Books, Cambridge
Tsoulfidis L, Tsaliki P (2014) Unproductive labour, capital accumulation and profitability crisis in the Greek economy. Int Rev Appl Econ 28(5):562–585
Webber M (1987) Quantitative measurement of some marxist categories. Environ Plan A 19(10):1303–1321
Wilcox R (2003) Applying contemporary statistical techniques. Gulf Professional Publishing, Houston